DIGGING INTO
CUSTER'S LAST STAND

Please direct correspondence or book orders
to the publisher at the following address:

AST Press
22 Todd Drive
Terre Haute, IN 47803
812-877-3691

Library of Congress Catalog Card Number
2003111929

ISBN 0-9745409-0-0 (cloth)
ISBN 0-9745409-1-9 (paper)

Printed by Citizen Printing Inc., Fort Collins, Colo.

CONTENTS

Digging Into Custer's Last Stand

INTRODUCTION

In late 1986, when my first edition of *Digging into Custer's Last Stand* was published, I had few expectations for it. I wanted to provide readers with a human interest account of the digs that would go beyond the technical books and articles the professional archeologists themselves would write and would focus on the human element behind the field work. I assumed my book would find its niche among students of the battle who also had some passing interest in the archeological activities at Little Bighorn. Time has proved how well I pegged my book's role — and how much I underestimated its popularity. While the battle audience has strongly supported the book over the years, it also has garnered appeal on a wider scale.

Equally surprising — and perhaps more satisfying personally — interest in archeology at Little Bighorn continues at a high level, even though more than 20 years have passed since a prairie fire scorched the Little Bighorn and set in motion a series of projects that have had a significant impact on our understanding of what took place on June 25-26, 1876.

The 1986 book focused solely on the fire of 1983, the archeological projects of 1984 and 1985, and the reburial service of 1986. That book was followed in 1990 by a sequel, *Shovels and Speculation, Archeologists Hunt Custer*. It offered a review of the 1989 project at Little Bighorn as well as similar, but unrelated, work at Fort Abraham Lincoln, south of Mandan, N. D., and the Custer Birthplace site in New Rumley, Ohio. In 1998, an expanded edition of *Digging into Custer's Last Stand* not only added new chapters about archeological activities at Little Bighorn in the 1990s but it also merged the chapters on the other Custer sites previously published in *Shovels and Speculation*, augmenting them with updated information.

This third edition of *Digging* is also expanded with new sections dealing with the Indian Memorial and the Horse Cemetery at Little Bighorn. Additional minor modifications have been made to the text and photographs in previously published sections throughout the book. Truly, that fire in 1983 at Little Bighorn continues to have a profound impact on the battlefield and its historical study.

Sandy Barnard
December 2003

Introduction, 1998 Edition

As a youngster, I always enjoyed the warmth and coziness of a crackling fire in our living room fireplace. My brothers and I would sit in front of the fireplace screen and conjure up all sorts of images we saw created by the leaping tongues of flame. Periodically, one of my parents would come by to remind us that Mr. Fire wasn't necessarily our friend. Keep the screen closed; sit back; don't touch. Fire, they reminded us, possessed a Jekyll-and-Hyde personality.

Today, as adults, we all understand the good side and bad side of fire. Who can forget the startling images of the fires that swept Yellowstone National Park in 1988? At the time, they seemed to be destroying the national treasure that Yellowstone is, but later we learned that fire often helps nature renew herself. Likewise, in 1983, many of us who feel a special bond with another National Park Service site, Little Bighorn Battlefield National Monument, were initially distressed when on Aug. 11, fire swept across its coulees and ridges in Montana. Fortunately, no one was hurt, no buildings or historical monuments were lost, and, as we have come to know, the battlefield ground itself was rejuvenated as nature intended. More important for our interest in history, that initial spark that soon became a conflagration led to studies that have had a profound effect upon our understanding and our interpretation of the great clash of cultures that began on a hot Sunday afternoon in June 1876 and continued through the next day. After the battle ended and the Sioux and Cheyenne had moved on, 268 white soldiers and civilians, including their commander, Lt. Col. George Armstrong Custer, lay dead on the field of combat. The Indian people carried away their own dead and wounded; the number killed or who later may have died exceeded 100.

Introduction

The previous edition of this book as well as its sequel, *Shovels & Speculation*, offered insight into the archeological projects that followed that 1983 fire. In 1984, 1985 and 1989, archeological teams, under the overall direction of Dr. Douglas D. Scott of the National Park Service's Midwest Archeological Center, combed the battlefield. At that time, archeologist Richard A. Fox, who was Scott's co-director of the battlefield digs, said, "Archeology is the physical evidence; history is the eyewitness testimony. Together they can solve a mystery."

As applied to the life and career of George Armstrong Custer, his words are proving insightful, if not fully correct. In the 1980s, in three areas of the country, separate groups working separately from each other came to a singular conclusion — that archeology could help unravel some of the mystery surrounding Custer and aspects of his life, including his final military engagement. The year 1997 marks the 121st anniversary of the Battle of the Little Bighorn, commonly known as Custer's Last Stand. The outline of Custer's final fight is familiar to many. On June 25, 1876, on a lonely treeless ridge above the Little Bighorn River, Lt. Col. George Armstrong Custer, arguably the best known soldier of his time, and some 209 men of his 7th U.S. Cavalry Regiment were killed in a classic engagement against an overwhelming number of Sioux and Cheyenne warriors. Four miles south, at what became known as the Reno-Benteen Defense Site, two of Custer's subordinates, Maj. Marcus A. Reno and Capt. Frederick Benteen, and about 350 of their troops successfully withstood a two-day siege by the same Indians who, unknown to them at the time, had wiped out Custer's force on June 25. Total army casualties amounted to 268. In the next section of this book, military history consultant Brian Pohanka offers an overview of the battle.

For the moment, we will note that Custer's actions that day have since been enshrouded in mystery and myth. The man's personality — flamboyant and laced with self-confidence — has prompted detractors to label him as bold but rash; other critics see in Custer the perfect symbol for what today are viewed as racist policies of the period visited upon the Indian tribes of this nation.

Somewhere, the individual separates from myth and symbol, and the historical figure emerges. That process of discovering the true Custer continues today, but probably is no closer to realization than in his own day. However, a little more than a decade ago, archeologists entered this often controversial, always befuddling picture of Custer and the Little Bighorn. In the 1980s, scientists examined three sites where Custer roamed in his lifetime:

• Then-Custer Battlefield National Monument in southeastern Montana: Major scientific inquiry was conducted at the place where the man died and his legend and myth were launched. In the 1980s, three archeological projects, funded by the Custer Battlefield Historical & Museum Association, were conducted at the National Park Service site.

    • Fort Abraham Lincoln, south of Mandan, N.D., and across the Missouri River from Bismarck, N.D.: If Little Bighorn marked the end of Custer's career, this frontier fort served as the jumping off point for other important events in his final three years, including the 1873 Yellowstone Expedition and the 1874 expedition which discovered gold in the Black Hills. During the late 1980s, archeological teams explored the site of the commanding officer's quarters at Fort Lincoln, the house that George and his wife, Libbie, called their home in North Dakota. In June 1989, a reconstruction of their house was dedicated. In the 1990s, three more buildings were reconstructed.

    • New Rumley, Harrison County, Ohio: The final scene of Custer-related archeological activity centered on his early life in this small rural hamlet at the site of the house where he was born Dec. 5, 1839.

    Enough time has passed for both formal historians as well as battle buffs (as opposed to Custer buffs) to assimilate the findings from the various projects, to think long about them, to debate them at countless public gatherings or over pizza and beer in private discussions, and, finally, to lay out new thoughts and interpretations. Foremost among them has been Rich Fox, the archeologist who assisted Scott during the early battlefield digs and led the projects at Fort Lincoln. After their field work ended, he retreated to think about the materials they had uncovered. Equally important, he closely studied Indian accounts, so often overlooked by those who study the battle. These stories had been dismissed for a variety of reasons, usually wrong-headed and even racist: Indians didn't think like whites so they couldn't explain clearly what had happened; white interpreters garbled the stories the Indians told; or, worse, the Indians' accounts weren't as relevant as what white soldiers had related about probably the most famous Indian-white battle in the 300 years of struggle in North America. Fox plunged into making sense of the tales the Indians had passed on. Then in his dissertation, he meshed their stories with the historical record of the white man as well as with the newly found archeological evidence. Eventually, his findings were published in his 1993 book, *Archeology, History and Custer's Last Battle*.

    As a result, Custeriana — or the study of the man himself and the battle that has been called popularly over the decades as Custer's Last Stand — has been stirred anew by his controversial theories. Although it is not my purpose to fully relate Fox's views, he essentially believes the soldiers did not put up the classic heroic struggle that whites have believed ever since 1876. He also outlines a quite different flow of battle that intrigues or repulses many buffs and has led to renewed argumentation about the events of 1876. In recent years, new books about Custer, his Indian opponents and their clash have continued to flow at a quick pace from the nation's publishing houses or from private efforts by individuals. At some point, each of these authors has had to consider Fox's theories, either adopting them, modifying them or rejecting them. In my own biography of one white casualty of the battle, *I Go With Custer, The Life and Death of Reporter Mark H. Kellogg*, I relied heavily on Fox in relating my own theories about Kellogg's personal demise on June 25, 1876. New biographies of Custer that have appeared in the 1990s by such noted writers as Robert M. Utley, Jeffry Wert and Louise Barnett have considered not only Fox but the archeological evidence that Scott and he developed more than a decade ago. The impact, indeed, has been profound.

Their efforts in the 1980s received reams of publicity at the time. I was fortunate to play a public relations role for the National Park Service during the 1985 and 1989 projects as well as the 1986 reburial service. Yet even though many years have passed since the reporters and their cameras departed the Little Bighorn, archeologists have remained busy at the site. The projects, including a substantial one in 1994, have been smaller and often conducted in a dimmer media spotlight. Partly as a result, these later findings have not been as widely distributed heretofore.

Thus, as the time neared to consider another reprint of my original *Digging Into Custer's Last Stand*, I decided instead to update my two original books by including information about these more recent projects. In addition, two other Custer sites which underwent unrelated archeological investigations in the late 1980s — Fort Abraham Lincoln near Mandan, N.D., and the Custer birthplace historical park in New Rumley, Ohio — also have changed since my book, *Shovels & Speculation*, which featured them, was published in 1990. Thus, this book includes much of the original material from my two earlier books. The original *Digging* material is featured in Chapter 3, while the *Shovels & Speculation* material is included in Chapters 3, 4 and 6. The new information in this 1998 version of this book can be categorized as follows:

   • An introductory battle overview, revised anew by Brian Pohanka, that takes into account new findings and interpretations applied to the Battle of Little Bighorn. This account replaces the one Pohanka offered in the first edition of *Digging Into Custer's Last Stand*.

Digging Into Custer's Last Stand

- The 1994 archeological project at Little Bighorn Battlefield National Monument. This was the largest project undertaken at the battlefield since those of the 1980s.

- Studies of remains discovered on the battlefield or previously buried in the Custer Battlefield National Cemetery.

- The private archeological efforts of rancher Jason Pitsch on his property in the Little Bighorn Valley, which includes much of the area of the opening attack by the 7th U.S. Cavalry under the command of Major Reno against the Sioux and Cheyenne village.

However, this book remains what its predecessors were — a mere introduction to the subject. This book does not seek to examine the full technical details of what the various teams of archeologists have uncovered. Instead, it will acquaint readers with efforts by the professional archeologists and volunteer groups seeking to preserve slices of history associated with Custer. Once acquainted with the subject, readers are encouraged to obtain not only Fox's earlier cited book, but also the two major technical books he wrote earlier with Scott, *Archaeological Perspectives on Battle of Little Bighorn* (1989) and *Archeological Insights Into the Custer Battle* (1987). For anyone who considers himself a battle buff, these three books should be considered must reading.

Since my two earlier dig books were published, one other major event has affected the modern Little Bighorn battlefield. In 1991, the U.S. Congress approved legislation renaming the NPS site from Custer Battlefield National Monument to Little Bighorn Battlefield National Monument. That makes consistent references to the park difficult and possibly may confuse some readers. Here is my approach to the problem: First, most of the material from the pre-1991 books has been included here, largely unchanged from its original publication. The battlefield in those years as well as earlier bore, in official as well in common usage, the name of George Armstrong Custer. In those earlier sections, references to "Custer Battlefield" remain. However, in material newly written for this book [1998], I use the congressionally approved name, whenever I refer to the modern NPS administrative site.

ACKNOWLEDGMENTS

This book began simply enough, after my first trip to Little Bighorn Battlefield National Monument in 1980. I soon found myself researching the life of *Bismarck Tribune* reporter Mark Kellogg, who perished with the Custer command on the main battlefield on June 25, 1876. As my research efforts broadened over the years, I have met many people who not only have assisted me with information and understanding of the events of 1876 but who have become my friends. Three have especially contributed to this book over the years: Brian Pohanka, a dig participant who, despite his own heavy schedule, offered his battle overview for this book; Jim Brust, who read the manuscript and always is willing to offer his advice; and Ron Nichols, also a dig participant whose keen analysis and close reading are always appreciated

At Little Bighorn Battlefield National Monument, a number of people associated with the National Park Service have graciously provided assistance to me over the years. Former Supt. Jim Court asked me to work with him in media relations during the 1985 dig and the 1986 reburial service. Without that opportunity to see the digs from the inside, this book would have been impossible. During that period, Chief Historian Neil Mangum provided me with my first behind the scenes insights into the battle and its personalities. More recently, between 1998-2002, Neil again provided all sorts of support and encouragement during his years as the battlefield's superintendent. Over the years their successors in both positions have continued to aid me whenever I have asked. Doug McChristian, Mangum's successor as historian, served as acting superintendent during the 1989 dig, my third stint in media relations at the NPS site. John Doerner, now chief historian, has continued to provide me with opportunities to gain insight through research in the NPS archives. I am especially indebted to archivist Kitty Belle Deernose, who always knows or can find exactly what I need to have for this or any of my other historical projects. During this period of continued archeological activity at Little Bighorn Battlefield, several other men and a woman have served as superintendent: Dennis Ditmanson, Barbara Suteer, Gerard Baker and, at present, Darrell Cook. Each welcomed me and made it easier for me to accomplish my work, for which I am most grateful. I would also like to thank Michael Stops, the battlefield's chief law enforcement officer, who has frequently allowed me to walk off the battlefield's trails for research and photo purposes.

In a separate category, but equally important, are the various archeologists and their supporting team of experts. This book would not have been possible without the willing support and guidance of Doug Scott, certainly one of the nicest and most unassuming men I have met in my nearly 35 years as a professional journalist. Also, I can't thank Richard Fox enough for his insights, both during the projects at the Little Bighorn as well as at Fort Abraham Lincoln. Over the years, Melissa Connor and Dick Harmon patiently answered my questions. Thanks, too, to the projects' forensic experts, Clyde Snow and P. Willey, as well as soils expert Vance Haynes.

At the Fort Lincoln Foundation, the two executive directors I have known over the years, Pat Ness and Tracy Potter, have willingly answered my questions about their projects, while at New Rumley, Ohio, Don Bier, archeologist with the Ohio Historical Society, assisted me as ably as his counterparts in the West. Jason Pitsch, a Garryowen, Mont., rancher, willingly shared not only information about his artifactual finds on his property but also his theories about the battle, especially the Valley Fight, much of which took place on his property.

Several other key people have provided me with support for this edition of the book or its predecessors. They are Cliff Hamby, Dan Martinez, James Woodcock, Ralph Heinz, Bill Armstrong, Glen Swanson and Trevis Mayfield, all of whom provided me with photos for the book. Todd Strand, former photo archivist at the State Historical Society of North Dakota, did likewise. Gary Raham drew my maps for the book. A special thanks goes to Jeff Broome, who also reviewed portions of my manuscript, Rick Collin and Darrell Dorgan. More recently, Jeff Hoffer, historian at Fort Abraham Lincoln State Park, has assisted me in updating the portion of the book dealing with that historic site. As always, I appreciate Jim Mundie's many words of encouragement and support.

One crucial group of folks cannot be overlooked and are most deserving of special praise. They are the men and women who worked as volunteers during one or more of the digs. During the projects I attended personally, they willingly shared their insights and anecdotes. Many later provided me with articles or other documents that enabled me to piece together the story of the digs, which is really their story.

During my research I have been privileged to befriend a number of the members of the Little Bighorn Associates and the Custer Battlefield Historical & Museum Association. To a man and to a woman, they are always willing to share their insights or to debate the finer points of the battle and its personalities. I would especially like to acknowledge the contributions of such folks as Father Vince Heier, Michael Donahue and the late Joe Sills.

Finally, and always, a special thanks to my wife, Betty, who continues to provide the love, support and understanding I need to complete my research and writing projects.

Digging Into Custer's Last Stand

Chapter One

REVISTING LITTLE BIGHORN

BY BRIAN POHANKA

On June 25, 1876, Lt. Col. George Armstrong Custer led the 7th U.S. Cavalry to disaster and immortality on the banks of a river his Indian opponents called the Greasy Grass. Ever since that fateful day the Battle of Little Bighorn — Custer's Last Stand — has provided a fascinating challenge to those who seek historical truth amid its overriding mystery.

Perhaps Col. William A. Graham, historian, author and longtime student of Little Bighorn, put it best when he wrote that "Custer's Last Fight has been the subject of more controversy, dissension, dispute and mendacity than almost any other event in American history....Almost everything about it is in some degree disputed." In the 122 years since warrior and soldier clashed on the vast, rolling prairie of southeastern Montana, many have attempted to reconstruct the fate of Custer's command, but no historian can ever hope to know every detail of the actual sequence and course of events.

Given the controversial circumstances and dramatic manner of his death, it is easy to forget that Custer's regiment was but one part of a larger military operation. The campaign that resulted in "The Great Sioux War" was designed to force so-called "hostiles" — principally Sioux (Lakota) and Cheyennes — to reservations, compelling them to forever abandon their traditional nomadic ways.

Three columns of soldiers advanced on the area believed to be occupied by what were assumed to be scattered bands of hostiles. From the west marched Col. John Gibbon's Montana Column; from the south came Brig. Gen. George Crook's Wyoming Column; and, from the east, beginning May 17, Brig. Gen. Alfred Terry started west from Fort Lincoln with his Dakota Column. Custer's 12-company 7th Cavalry, some 600 strong, made up the bulk of Terry's force.

Digging Into Custer's Last Stand

Unbeknownst to the Army commanders, their opponents, numbering as many as 10,000 men, women and children, had coalesced under the leadership of the charismatic Hunkpapa medicine man Sitting Bull. On June 17, as Terry and Custer headed westward from the confluence of the Powder and Yellowstone rivers toward a junction with Gibbon's command, Crook's column was attacked near the Rosebud River by a large force of Sioux. Although the Indians were driven off after a day-long battle and casualties on both sides were light, Crook curtailed his northward march.

Four days later, at the mouth of the Rosebud, Terry, Gibbon and Custer, unaware of Crook's defeat, planned their next move. A nine-day scout of six companies, led by Custer's second-in-command, Maj. Marcus A. Reno, brought word that an estimated 800 warriors were headed in the direction of the Little Bighorn River. In view of Custer's daring nature and experience in Indian warfare, Terry accorded him the honor of pursuing the Indians south, up the Rosebud, then west to the headwaters of the Little Bighorn. Meanwhile Terry and Gibbon would march west along the Yellowstone, then south along the Big Horn River to the mouth of the Little Bighorn. If all went well, Terry would arrive at that point on June 26, ready to entrap whatever hostiles Custer had pressured from the south. Unfortunately for Terry's plans, Indian strength had grown considerably, and the loose coalition of tribes encamped on Little Bighorn included somewhere between 1,500 and 3,000 adult warriors.

Travelling light, Custer's regiment — 597 soldiers plus 50 scouts and civilians — advanced rapidly up the Rosebud hindered only by the slower mule-borne pack train. By June 24, Custer's Crow and Ree scouts had determined that a large Indian village was likely situated on the lower reaches of the Little Bighorn. After a cautious night march, Custer joined his scouts at 9 a.m. Sunday, June 25, atop a rocky crest known as the "Crow's Nest." The scouts told Custer that they had spotted a huge hostile encampment 15 miles distant in the valley of Little Bighorn. Although Custer himself could not make out the village and its massive pony herd, he accepted his scouts' information.

Concerned that his regiment had been spotted by outriding Indian hunting parties and fearing that his elusive foe would scatter, Custer decided to risk a daylight attack rather than wait to strike at dawn as he had in the Battle of the Washita eight years earlier. Uncertain of the exact disposition of his quarry, Custer dispatched Capt. Frederick Benteen and the 115 men of Companies D, H and K with orders to ride southward, over a succession of ridges to the river valley, and strike outlying villages that might be located there. Should Benteen find no villages, he was to countermarch to rejoin the rest of the command.

Two hours and several miles closer to the Little Bighorn, Custer further divided his command. He ordered Major Reno to cross the river and attack what he feared was already a scattering foe. Reno's battalion included 35 scouts and the 140 troopers of Companies A, G and M. Custer himself, with Companies C, E, F, I and L — some 220 men prior to the dispatch of messengers and straggling of men whose horses gave out — moved northward up the high bluffs and rugged ground east of the river.

The pack mules, escorted by 135 men including Capt. Thomas McDougall's Company B, lagged far to the rear and would rejoin the command only after the Indians had been engaged.

We will never know for certain what Custer intended. Sgt. Daniel Kanipe, who soon after was sent back with a message urging on the pack train, said the move was a pursuit of 50 or more warriors who had materialized on the flanks of the bluff. Perhaps Custer feared their presence indicated that a hostile force had already sallied forth to engage the soldiers; or he may have intended to follow them into the village proper. Cheyenne accounts confirm the presence of this group, which included the warriors Wolf Tooth and Big Foot. Some historians think it likely that Custer was endeavoring to cut off the supposed flight of his prey — Interpreter Frederick Gerard informed Custer that

Lt. Col. George Armstrong Custer
(Little Bighorn Battlefield National Monument)

he had spotted the Indians "running like devils." Other students of the battle believe Custer planned to hit the village at its northern end in a classic pincer movement. Like so many aspects of Little Bighorn, the fatal move northward is shrouded in mystery and controversy.

Almost immediately Custer's hastily improvised plans began to go awry. Although the Indians had in fact been taken by surprise, hundreds of warriors — fiercely determined to safeguard their panicked families — sallied forth to confront Reno's advance. Alarmed at the growing numbers in his front and the vast Indian village that lay to the north, Reno halted his battalion, dismounted, and formed a skirmish line. The led horses were taken into a belt of timber that lay along the river on Reno's right flank, and with one company detached to safeguard the mounts, the major's line risked being surrounded. After 10 to 15 minutes of fighting, Reno drew his exposed companies back into the cover of the trees. Although Custer had assured Reno that his advance would be supported, and the major had dispatched two couriers alerting his commander to the fact that the warriors were coming forth in strength to confront the soldiers' attack, Custer's battalion was obviously not in supporting distance.

Half an hour later, with Indian pressure increasing and warriors infiltrating Reno's perimeter on all sides, the shaken major ordered his soldiers to mount, and launched a charge from the timber. It was a fighting retreat that quickly degenerated into a panicked rout, desperate troopers galloping for the river and the 200-foot high bluffs beyond with howling warriors in hot pursuit.

Digging Into Custer's Last Stand

THE DAILY GRAPHIC

NEW YORK, MONDAY, JULY 10, 1876.

George Armstrong Custer
(Sandy Barnard)

By the time Reno's exhausted survivors had gained the summit, 90 of the battalion's 175 men were dead, wounded or missing.

Meanwhile, having called off his foray to the south, Captain Benteen followed the trail of the other companies, enroute receiving two messages from Custer urging him to the scene of action. About 4:20 p.m., as the last of Reno's defeated troopers were gaining the bluffs east of the Little Bighorn, Benteen made his appearance. A little more than half an hour later, the first of Captain McDougall's pack mules began to arrive. While Benteen supervised the establishment of a defensive perimeter, the Indian pressure abated and heavy firing was heard to the north. Clearly Custer was engaged.

Disturbed that neither of his superiors seemed interested in riding to the sound of Custer's guns, at 4:45 p.m. Captain Thomas Weir started his Company D north from the defensive site. This unauthorized move prompted a poorly coordinated advance by the remaining companies, several units joining Weir's troopers atop a high ridge known today as Weir Point. This position was one mile north of Reno's perimeter and three miles from the spot where Custer met his death. It is likely that Weir's men unknowingly witnessed the very last stages of Custer's battle.

By 6 p.m., the sight of approaching Indians compelled the exposed companies to retire to their initial position on the bluffs. Only one man (Farrier Vincent Charley of Company D) was lost in the disorganized withdrawal, largely thanks to the efforts of Lt. Edward S. Godfrey, who conducted a fighting retreat with the dismounted skirmishers of Company K. As Reno's and Benteen's men dug in for a protracted siege, some harbored misgivings about the fate of Custer's command, though most were convinced that he had pulled off to the north in the direction of Terry's forces.

For the remainder of June 25 and all through the 26th, the seven companies endured a deadly sniping fire that claimed the lives of 18 more men. In a hollow swale at the center of the position, Dr. Henry R. Porter cared for the battalion's wounded amid the shambles of the pack train. When canteens were emptied, water could be obtained only by harrowing forays back down the bluffs to the river below. Few Indians dared to attack the fortified position, and those that did venture too close were charged and scattered by a detachment led by Captain Benteen. Indeed, it was Benteen, rather than the shaken Reno, who maintained the unit's morale and oversaw the successful defense.

By the night of June 26, the attackers had slowly faded away, and by dawn the surviving soldiers were able to breathe more easily. At 11 a.m. June 27, Terry's and Gibbon's column came into view, marching through the detritus of the abandoned Indian village. But the rescued troopers' joy was short-lived; Custer's slain battalion had been discovered downstream.

On June 28, the 7th Cavalry buried its dead. The fatal battlefield confronted them with what Lieutenant Godfrey called "a scene of sickening, ghastly horror." Scattered over the sagebrush-covered ridges and coulees were the bodies of all 210 officers and men who had ridden into the final fight with Custer's contingent. Most were naked; many had been terribly mutilated. "It would be impossible to put into print the sight that met our eyes at that place," Sgt. Charles Windolph later wrote. "They were simply unspeakable in their nature."

In later years many survivors were understandably reticent about what they found on Custer's battlefield. But it is from their testimony, plus interviews with Indian participants and artifacts found on the site, that historians have attempted to piece together the movements of the five doomed companies. In recent years scholars have been fortunate to be able to draw from the extensive writings of Walter Mason Camp, an incomparably dedicated researcher who sought out and interviewed dozens of Little Bighorn veterans. Little known to earlier authors, Camp has now been deservedly recognized as the most important of all early 20th century students of the battle.

The last man to see Custer alive left the battalion about 3:20 p.m. when a young Italian-born trumpeter named Giovanni Martini departed with a message for Benteen. Hastily scrawled by Custer's adjutant, the note read, "Benteen — Come on. Big village. Be quick. Bring packs. W.W. Cooke. P.S. Bring pacs [sic]." The trumpeter left Custer as the head of the column was about to enter the valley at Medicine Tail Coulee.

While Martini's recollections were sometimes contradictory, Custer apparently followed Medicine Tail Coulee toward the river and village 1 1/4 miles to the west. Martini told of a party of Indians — possibly part of the group Custer had spotted earlier — who fired on the rear of the column; one of their bullets wounded the trumpeter's horse. In the 1940s, Custer Battlefield Supt. Edward Luce discovered a line of expended carbine shells that would seem to confirm an initial engagement at this point. Martini also described passing Custer's brother, Boston, who had ridden overland from the pack train to join the battalion in the coming fight. Boston Custer would surely have informed his brother of the relative proximity of Benteen's column, which he had passed along the way.

Several Indian accounts describe an attempt spearheaded by Company E (the Gray Horse Troop) to ford the river at the mouth of Medicine Tail Coulee, opposite the Cheyenne circle at the northern edge of the village — an attack "repulsed" by a determined handful of young Cheyennes. Some students of the battle believe the movement of a portion of Custer's force to the ford was a feint, intended to pin warriors in place while the remainder of his command continued northward to flank the village from that direction. Others, including Richard Fox in his 1993 study, *Archaeology, History and Custer's Last Battle*, postulate that since the encampment had emptied of fleeing non-combatants by the time Custer approached the ford, a movement north to intercept the fugitives made more sense than charging into a largely abandoned village.

In the 122 years since the battle, artifacts indicating an action of some kind have been found in the vicinity of the ford, though their relative paucity seems to indicate the fighting there was brief. However, beginning in the 1920s, several hundred soldier shell cases have been found on high ground some 1,000 yards to the north and east. The discovery of this position, variously known as Blummer or Nye-Cartwright Ridge, indicates that all or part of Custer's command passed over this ground enroute to the final battlefield. According to a number of surviving 7th Cavalrymen, Custer had earlier divided his battalion into two smaller wings or squadrons, commanded by Captains Myles Keogh and George Yates.

Thus it is quite possible that while one squadron (generally assumed to have been Companies E and F under Yates' command) approached the ford, the other three companies, under Keogh, moved northward along the crest of Blummer/Nye-Cartwright Ridge. Clearly some sort of engagement occurred here, but since only a handful of slain soldiers were later found in the vicinity, the firing was likely at fairly long range. The decisive battle would come more than a half a mile to the north.

Some historians assume Custer's movement away from the ford to have been a beleaguered withdrawal under heavy pressure from his warrior foes. Others believe that at least a portion of the battalion lingered on the ridge overlooking the ford, awaiting the arrival of Benteen's command, before riding to the fatal battleground. A more likely scenario, given Custer's aggressive temperament, interprets his north-ward progress as a continuation of his offensive strategy. Archeological evidence seems to lend support to Cheyenne oral tradition describing a rapid movement by part of Custer's command, probably Yates' squadron, to the vicinity of another

Custer Battlefield National Cemetery with Last Stand Hill in the background,
by Ken Roahan, c. 1940
(Little Bighorn Battlefield National Monument)

ford, northwest of the present-day museum and National Cemetery. According to this interpretation, it was only when warrior pressure began to mount against the three companies of Captain Keogh's command, deployed near what is known today as Calhoun Hill, that Custer was finally forced to wage a desperate — and brief — defensive battle.

Many Indian accounts credit the Cheyenne war leader Lame White Man with launching a decisive charge that precipitated the rapid collapse of the soldier position. This attack may have come in response to the deployment of Company C from the vicinity of Calhoun Hill to a position closer to the river, where the troopers became a vulnerable target for Lame White Man's assault. This sudden reversal turned the tables on Custer's command and brought the soldiers on Calhoun Hill under heavy pressure from front and flank. Other warriors moved along the cover of ridges to the east and took Keogh's Company I under fire before those troopers could adequately react to the unfolding disaster. With every fourth trooper detailed as a horse-holder for his own mount and those of three comrades, the dismounted company skirmish lines were dangerously thin, while the led horses presented a vulnerable target to warriors attempting to stampede them.

In his testimony before an Army court of inquiry investigating Reno's conduct at Little Bighorn, Captain Benteen asserted that the scattered disposition of the dead on Custer's field showed the clash to have been "a rout, a panic, till the last man was killed." Others shared this view. Pvt. Jacob Adams later wrote, "We came to the conclusion then and there that the fight had been a rout, a running fight."

Many of the later Indian accounts confirm this impression of chaos, rapid disintegration and annihilation. "Horses were running over the soldiers and over each other," the Cheyenne Wolftooth remembered. "The fighting was really close and they were shooting almost without taking aim." Low Dog, an Oglala war leader, likewise recalled his opponents "did very poor shooting." In an apparent reference to the horse holders, Low Dog noted, "Their horses were so frightened that they pulled the men all around, and a great many of their shots went up in the air and did us no harm."

Benteen claimed to have counted some 70 dead cavalry horses on Custer's battleground, and only two dead Indian ponies — not unlikely given the fact that the Sioux and Cheyennes generally preferred stealthy infiltration to head-on mounted assaults — but also, perhaps, lending credence to the view that the troopers were wiped out before they were able to assume a cohesive defensive position. Many scholars believe that no more than 50 Indians died in the Custer battle, and some have set the figure at less than 40. The fact that the Indians were able to remove their dead from the field has added to the continuing debate over the number of warrior casualties.

The first significant concentration of soldier dead was found at the southwestern corner of the battlefield, and included some 15 troopers, among them Sergeants Jeremiah Finley and August Finckle of Company C. On the rise northeast of this position lay men of Company L, including Custer's brother-in-law, Lt. James Calhoun, for whom the hill was later named. A number of witnesses reported that Calhoun's men appeared to have been deployed in skirmish formation, and around some bodies were scattered 25 to 40 expended carbine shells. Clearly Calhoun's troopers had put up a fight.

On the exposed eastern slope of battle ridge, halfway between Calhoun Hill and the site of "Custer's Last Stand," Captain Keogh's body was identified amidst a pile of slain troopers. One of his trumpeters was sprawled across the captain's corpse, and several of his non-commissioned officers lay nearby. Most of the dead men in this group seemed to have belonged to Keogh's Company I, though First Sgt. Edwin Bobo of Company C was among the number. The remains of men from several companies were scattered up the slope from Keogh's position toward Last Stand Hill.

Atop the ridge, and scattered down the western slope, were the bodies of George Custer, Capt. Thomas Custer of Company C (the General's brother, who was likely serving as an aide that day), Regimental Adjutant Cooke, and the bulk of Captain Yates' Company F. Yates and his subordinate officer, Second Lt. William Van Wyck Reily, were there, as was First Lt. Algernon Smith of Company E. Several witnesses noted a body believed to be that of Surgeon George E. Lord was also among the dead at this point. Lieutenant Godfrey stated that 42 slain troopers were found with Custer on the hill, along with 39 dead horses that appeared to have been killed to form an impromptu barricade. From all appearances Custer had chosen to make a "last stand" at this point.

The only other large concentration of dead was found several hundred yards southwest of Custer Hill in the upper recesses of a deep ravine leading to the river. Numerous witnesses counted 28 bodies there, among whom were First Sgt. Frederick Hohmeyer and five others identified as belonging to Company E, the "Gray Horse Troop." Several men from Company F were also tentatively identified in the vicinity of "Deep Ravine." While most of these dead were assumed to be from Company E, here, as elsewhere on the field, mutilation and decomposition made positive identifications difficult, if not impossible. Whether their location indicated a tactical deployment or doomed flight, at some point these troopers had been cut off and forced to wage their own last stand in what one witness called "a veritable cul de sac."

Scattered bodies — Captain McDougall said no more than a dozen — were found between the ravine and Custer Hill. Near the foot of the hill lay the commanding officer's brother, civilian Boston Custer, and his nephew Arthur Reed. On the flats, a "stone's throw from the river," the body of another civilian, news reporter Mark H. Kellogg of the *Bismarck (Dakota Territory) Tribune*, was discovered by Colonel Gibbon.This was the mute testimony of disaster. Unfortunately for future historians, no detailed, accurate maps were made showing the location of the dead men and horses, or of the carbine shells scattered about the field. Indeed, no one was ever quite sure how many corpses were interred on Custer's battleground. Most witnesses seem to have shared the sentiments of Capt. Walter Clifford of Gibbon's 7th Infantry who wrote in his diary, "Let us bury our dead and flee from this rotting atmosphere."

For today's visitor one of the most obvious features of Little Bighorn National Monument are the marble markers that dot the rolling landscape. These purport to show where the soldier dead were found and originally buried, and have provided a primary ingredient to many historical studies of the Last Stand. But just how accurate are they? Like many aspects of Little Bighorn, from the beginning the subject is clouded in controversy. Contemporary records of the number of dead interred on Custer's battlefield vary from 202 to 212, with most estimates falling in the range of 204 to 208. So few shovels were available that these internments were hasty and inadequate at best. In most cases the remains were either rolled into shallow excavations, or simply covered with dirt scooped up from either side of the body. A wooden stake was pounded at the head of each burial, and then the Army departed.

In the summer of 1877 a detail returned to the battlefield with orders to disinter the remains of slain officers for shipment to their families. Even in Custer's case identification was difficult. Heavy rains, melting snow and scavenging animals had opened many of the graves, and the bones of horses and men were intermingled. Eventually eight bodies were removed from the Custer portion of the field and three from the Reno/Benteen site. At his father's request Second Lt. John J. Crittenden was re-interred on Calhoun Hill at the spot where he fell. The bodies of four other officers could not be located or identified. While part of the detail went about this grim task, others reburied the disinterred remains of enlisted men, again marking the spots as best they could. Shortly after the detail departed, photographer John Fouch arrived on the scene and took the earliest known image of Last Stand Hill.

Two years later, Capt. George K. Sanderson led another detachment to the field and reburied numerous human bones. He then gathered all the horse bones he could find and placed them inside a large stack of cordwood on the crest of Custer Hill. Photographer Stanley J. Morrow made a number of images of this 1879 expedition.

In July 1881, First Lt. Charles F. Roe supervised the erection of an 18-ton granite shaft bearing the names of the soldier dead. Around the memorial, which was set in place at the site of the former cordwood marker atop Custer Hill, Roe's detachment interred as many human remains as they could locate in a mass grave. Before the detail departed, a civilian scout named James Campbell allegedly restaked the original grave sites to preserve the locations where the troopers had fallen five years before.

In April 1890, with Campbell's guidance another soldier detachment traveled to Little Bighorn. Their commander, Capt. Owen J. Sweet, supervised the installation of the marble markers that now dot the battlefield. Unfortunately for future historians, Campbell and Sweet erected 249 stones while only 210 men died with Custer's battalion. Whether the surplus markers were intended for Reno's battleground — where the graves had never been adequately marked — or because depressions and clumps of foliage were interpreted as former burial sites, the damage had been done. According to Sweet's report, the captain seems to have been under the impression that he was actually marking graves, not the locations of former burials. In fact, Sweet's contingent did find human bones at many of the marker sites — indication that the earlier reburial detail had overlooked portions of soldier remains.

Digging Into Custer's Last Stand

7th Cavalry Monument,
Last Stand Hill
**(Little Bighorn Battlefield
National Monument)**

Modern-day surveys have plotted a total of 242 markers on the Custer battlefield, seven less than Sweet installed in 1890, but still 32 more than the historical record indicates should be there.

Further complicating the puzzle is the fact that Sweet did not install markers for civilians Kellogg, Boston Custer and Reed, while in 1910 four more stones were set up for the missing or unidentified officers: Lieutenants Porter, Harrington and Sturgis, and Surgeon Lord.

Prior to the 1984 and 1985 archeological surveys, a general impression existed of where the spurious markers were located. Among the more obvious examples is Custer Hill, where today 52 stones occupy a site where 43 bodies were discovered. Another is the line of more than 50 markers between Custer Hill and Deep Ravine, where several observers said no more than a dozen bodies were found. This so-called "South Skirmish Line" has been one of the most hotly debated features of the Custer battle.

But perhaps the most baffling error was one of omission. No stones were erected in Deep Ravine where almost every contemporary witness described a concentration of 28 or more dead. Some students of Little Bighorn believe at least some of these dead were removed from the depression, while others think their remains are yet to be found, somewhere in the winding recesses of the ravine. One author has even suggested that the 28 bodies were never in this particular ravine at all.

These were but a few of the tantalizing mysteries of Custer's Last Stand that awaited archeological investigation in the summer of 1983.

Chapter Two

ARCHEOLOGICAL SURVEYS

AT CUSTER BATTLEFIELD

1984-1985

Archeologist Richard Fox measures a section of soil well below the surface of Deep Ravine while geomorphologist Vance Haynes records the data during the May 1985 archeological project at then-Custer Battlefield National Monument.

(Sandy Barnard)

Digging Into Custer's Last Stand

TROOPER MIKE S DISCOVERY

Dr. Jim Thorpen poked, gently, with his dental pick at the hard-baked Montana prairie dirt surrounding the yellowed human leg bone.

"See there!" the husky pathologist from Casper, Wyo., said, his voice jumping. Beyond his pick a two-inch ridge of black leather peeked from beneath the dirt, a few inches from the bone.

"I'll bet when we finish clearing away the dirt, we'll find the bones still attached to that boot," Thorpen said, tipping back his broad-brim cowboy hat.

In a few minutes his prediction proved accurate.

"That boot and the bones in there are in the soldier's death position, the way they were when the Indians killed him," Thorpen explained, as he tenderly wisked dirt from his find. His voice was barely audible as a 30 mile-an-hour wind swallowed his words on a chilly day, despite the high sun, late in May 1985 at the Custer Battlefield National Monument.

Later, archeologist Melissa Connor, whose straight blonde hair and plastic-framed glasses belied her gritty devotion to her task of directing the excavation at Marker 128, echoed Thorpen's comments.

Peering at the jumbled bones uncovered nearby in a 6-inch hole on Greasy Grass Ridge, Connor said, "Those bones are the most complete human remains we've found in the two years of digs at the Custer Battlefield."

Nearly 110 years before, on a June day described as brassy hot, a soldier, probably a member of Company C of the 7th U.S. Cavalry, fought his personal last fight at that spot and died. Volunteer Pat Phillips, a University of Nebraska, Lincoln, graduate student who studied the artifacts in the laboratory, labeled him "Trooper Mike" because his remains were found in excavation square "M." Two mushroomed bullets mixed with the bones underscored the violence of his life's end.

FIRE SWEEPS CUSTER BATTLEFIELD

Throughout the summer of 1983 Custer Battlefield crackled under the feet of the thousands of tourists who walked the historic grounds. Rain seldom disturbed them as they wondered about what had happened one summer afternoon in 1876.

In late June, at a lunch served to members of the Little Big Horn Associates at the Reno Crossing below the Reno-Benteen Defense Site, Battlefield Supt. Jim Court expressed his growing concern. In his five years at the battlefield he had never seen the ridges and coulees so tinder dry.

Still, prairie vegetation, well-adapted to drought conditions, was thriving, having nearly reached the top of the 3-foot marble markers. Growth was especially heavy on the east side of Battle Ridge where Capt. Myles Keogh's Company I had been overwhelmed.

By mid-August, conditions were ripe for fire. On Aug. 9, a grass fire scorched the ground north of the battlefield along U.S. Highway 212, but employees of the Crow Indian Tribe and the Bureau of Indian Affairs thought they had checked the blaze that consumed some 100 acres. One BIA employee said, "We thought we had it out. We had doused every smoke."

Archeological Surveys at Custer Battlefield 1984-1985

Earth may rumble; rampaging water can sweep away whatever lies in its path. But fire, to man, is special. When it is controlled, it can warm him, cook his food, give him light. Out of control, it terrifies him. Overnight on the 9th, the fire slept. By 11 a. m. Wednesday Aug. 10, it roused, and this time, driven by high winds, it would not be slowed as it moved onto the battlefield proper.

"This land has not been grazed for 90 years," Court recalled. Parched, the national historic site was a fire bomb awaiting a spark to unleash its fury.

Maintenance Chief Bill Hartung, now retired, recalled that "When it started, there was no hope, nothing to do but to run for your life."

Fighting Fire at Custer Battlefield

In the summer of 1983, the late John Parle, an unpretentious fellow from Santa Clara, Calif., was eager to start his second "career" as a volunteer-in-park at Custer Battlefield. The summer job was a dream come true for the recently retired sheet metal worker.

"I first became interested in General Custer as a 9-year-old boy in Santa Clara," recalled Parle, in his mid-60s. "I saw a picture of the Battle of the Little Bighorn in a store window and it fascinated me. I used to stop on my way to and from school and look at it."

Still, he never expected his first season as a ranger to be so exciting. "I may have been the first to spot the fire," he believes.

By 11 the morning of Aug. 10, he had finished a talk to tourists on Custer Hill by the black iron fence which surrounds the spot where Custer's marker stands today.

"When I got done with my presentation, a big wind was blowing. I walked down to the museum and they sent me to the Deep Ravine trail head to get the money for the brochures out of the coin box. When I was there, I saw a big cloud of smoke coming up from behind Calhoun Hill."

He hollered to Park Technician Mardell Plainfeather, "It looks as if the fire from yesterday has started up."

In charge because Court and Chief Historian Neil Mangum were away, she told him, "Go up on the hill and see what you can see."

Parle recalls, "When I got on the monument site, I could see the fire sweeping over the back of Calhoun Hill across

John Parle was on duty the day fire struck Little Bighorn Battlefield National Monument in August 1983.

(Sandy Barnard)

Digging Into Custer's Last Stand

The 1983 fire seared many of the 7th Cavalry markers on the field, but did not cause them any lasting damage.
(Dan Martinez)

the road and down toward the river. A few minutes later Bill Hartung and Cliff Arbogast, who's now the maintenance chief, came over to me and told me to get the people off the hill, because by then the fire was coming toward the hill."

Then the two maintenance men disappeared through the smoke. "I had seen some campers and stuff going down the ridge toward the river and I knew they would be behind the fire line."

Parle quickly turned to clearing the monument. "I started telling people to get off the hill but they didn't want to go. Some of them took their own sweet time about it. The fire was getting pretty close and they're all standing there taking pictures."

While on the hill, he observed seasonal ranger Chris Summitt, whom he calls the "Big Hero of the day," head down Deep Ravine trail, disappear into the smoke and come out with four people.

"A little later I saw him go back in and come out with two more. There were some people down there who didn't know about the fire and would have been trapped."

Back down at the museum, he could see flames, 15 feet high and a half mile long, moving closer to the map room. Plainfeather told him to clear the main parking lot. She feared big spruce trees ringing the national cemetery would soon be ablaze and spread flames to vehicles in the parking lot. If gasoline tanks exploded, a worse disaster could result.

"They started calling out on the loud speaker but again, it was hard to get people to move. They were just lollygagging about it to the point where we had to tell them to move or we would have to cite them."

Next, Parle headed for the park's main gate to block incoming traffic. Despite the danger, tourists were still trying to get into the battlefield. "I closed the gate but I had to open it frequently to let big equipment through. Bull dozers and people from other fire departments."

After about 40 minutes, Parle headed for the government living quarters below the Stone House where other park personnel and he lived. "I saw fire come around the edge of the quarters down by the maintenance building. I headed down because I had to retrieve my money and my car from the house at the end of the driveway.

"Luck was with us that day," Parle recalls. "Luckily just two days before Cliff Arbogast had given us a course on how to use the fire hoses. I started dragging fire hoses out and got one going and started wetting my house and the others down."

Other park personnel, including Tim Bernadis, Gary Johnson and Danny Plainfeather, also helped soak the buildings. Janitor John Bird in Ground turned on the sprinklers. Fortunately, too, the stiff wind began blowing the fire away from the buildings. "Otherwise it would have burned us all out."

In the cemetery itself the fire did only minimal damage, scorching trees on the east end of the battlefield overlook. But the battlefield itself was another story. "It was as black as a freeway. I had no idea when I went to the battlefield that summer that anything like that would happen," Parle said, "but when it was over, I realized the fire was a pretty spectacular event. It was the talk of the town for a long time afterwards."

The fire-fighting effort took much of the day. "It was 5:30 before we were all finished with it. It burned right down to the river and the roots of the sagebrush were still smoldering.

A CHAIN OF FORTUITOUS CIRCUMSTANCES

A fire is a calamity, and everyone feared that was the case with the blaze that gave the Custer Battlefield the appearance of what Jim Court called "a Safeway parking lot." Actually, it turned out to be one more link in a chain of fortuitous circumstances that has led to significant knowledge about the Custer battle.

"In the long run, the fire is the best thing that ever happened to this place," Court believes.

The 1983 fire burned off most of the vegetation on the battlefield and left it blackened.
(Dan Martinez)

Digging Into Custer's Last Stand

The first link occurred in 1978 when Court, a veteran National Park Service administrator, arrived as superintendent for Custer Battlefield National Monument. Since then, he had pushed for some formal battlefield study. He knew many artifacts had been recovered in and around the battlefield, but no one ever had undertaken a controlled survey to determine what historical materials might lurk beneath the prairie surface. He also considered the marble markers the most distinctive feature at the battlefield, one that causes it to stand out among all the places American troops have fought because they designate where soldiers fell. But their accuracy, questionable at best, needed checking, Court believed.

Court, a frank man who seldom hides his opinions, speaks simply about why he had long badgered his employers to let a project be done: "I was curious about what we could find."

Equally curious was Neil Mangum, a transplanted Virginian whose assignment in 1980 as battlefield historian enabled him to realize one of his personal goals by his early 30s.

In the fire's aftermath, both men realized they had an unprecedented opportunity to have the grass and sage-covered battle grounds studied in a way never before possible, if they could act fast. Fortunately, luck was with them. Home on summer vacation was the son of one of Court's neighbors in Hardin, Rich Fox, then a doctoral candidate in archeology at the University of Calgary in Alberta, Canada.

Better known as "Rabbit," Fox quickly assented to survey grounds which he had roamed many times as a youngster. On Aug. 19, 1983, just nine days after the fire, he met with Court and Mangum to develop research objectives for his study, which he conducted in the field from Aug. 23 to Sept. 2. His chief purpose was to determine whether archeological techniques could produce physical data to aid the historical interpretation of the battle.

In the field, Fox, a bear of a man who loves to finish off a day of hot field work with a six pack, found a remarkable number of metal artifacts and bone materials, plus some intriguing mounds in Deep Ravine. In his November, 1983, report he recommended "implementation of an archeological sampling program to further assess the potential of archeology in shedding light on historical problems and providing data to augment public interpretative programs."

Several specific steps that he called for ultimately formed the research basis for the 1984 and 1985 field work. They were:

- Exploration of Deep Ravine through excavation and trenching to determine whether any bodies are still there.
- Recovery and analysis of battlefield artifacts to determine patterns of soldier and Indian movements that might reveal information about the flow of combat action.
- Field study to determine correlation between present marker sites and actual historic burial locations. Marker 33 on the South Skirmish Line area drew particular attention because a park visitor had found human remains there. Fox later uncovered more at that spot.

A secondary recommendation calling for "an interdisciplinary approach" to archeological investigations at Custer Battlefield also proved important later, when

16

various specialists were invited to join the archeological team. Court could not have been more enthusiastic about the recommendations, but he faced a dilemma. The NPS had no funds for such an ambitious undertaking.

Doug Scott - Right Place at the Right Time

On Dec. 5, 1983, Dr. Douglas D. Scott was excited about his new job as supervisory archeologist for the NPS Midwest Archeological Center in Lincoln, Neb. One of his first tasks was to review a draft of the post-fire Custer Battlefield study by Fox.

A look at his calendar caused Scott to chuckle. The date—Dec. 5—was Custer's birthday. "A little irony there that does not escape me."

In Fox's report he found "a lot of potential from an archeological point of view. The question was — should more be done and when and by whom? It was a management decision ultimately."

Archeologists Melissa Connor and Doug Scott testing a sophisticated electronic transit within the fence enclosure of Last Stand Hill in May 1985.

(Sandy Barnard)

Should Fox direct a follow-up project? That decision was easy. The battlefield's own high profile dictated that NPS run its own project.

"So I was designated to do it," said Scott, whose background is in historical archeology and military history. Scott also is highly knowledgeable about frontier period firearms.

A modest man, he terms his appointment to explore Custer Battlefield as merely "one of those acts of fate. I happened to come in at the right place at the right time."

He also insisted that Fox play an important role. "It would have been ludicrous — personally and professionally — to have dumped Rich — to have said this is strictly a park service project. I don't like to work that way." Besides, by February 1984, as field planning became more intense, "We realized that many of our ideas were similar and that we could work together."

They knew, too, the project would have to rely heavily on volunteer labor, because no government funding was available to hire a professional crew. The park service would cover Scott's salary but money for Fox, supplies and other costs would come from the non-profit Custer Battlefield Historical & Museum Association.

Relying on volunteers didn't bother Scott, who had worked with them on other projects. "It was a way to get the job done in an expeditious way and to stimulate the public interest."

Gradually, through late 1983 and early 1984 plans took shape. At the battlefield, Court prepared for something he had pushed for since 1978. Word went forth that volunteers were needed to assist the archeologists.

Meanwhile, in Lincoln, Scott, coordinating with Fox, developed a three-fold research plan for the 765 acres under NPS control (Most of the 9,000 acres on which the troops and Indians fought are in private hands). First, the main battlefield and the Reno-Benteen site would be searched by visual reconnaissance to locate artifacts that Scott expected "would be on the surface for the picking up." Suspecting also that many metallic artifacts would be buried, they decided to back up the visual survey with metal detector operations.

Secondly, a systematic search by digging 2 x 2 meter squares would be conducted at a random sample of 10 percent of the numerous markers, thought at the time to number about 250. This would test one theory: Did locations having two markers represent only one actual burial site? Finding artifacts or bones in a square would indicate a soldier had once rested there.

Finally, perhaps most intriguing, were 28 men of Company E still buried in Deep Ravine? Both archeologists had their own theories but kept their minds open. Perhaps a dig would prove which of countless theories was accurate.

RISING EXPECTATIONS FOR THE CUSTER DIG

As the May 7 start for the five-week project approached, Scott and Fox found their preparations gaining increased public and media attention. Discussion focused on two possibilities: That the battlefield's century-old mysteries might at last be unraveled and the missing Company E troopers might be located in Deep Ravine.

As early as Feb. 15, Neil Mangum sought to quiet unrealistic speculation, telling *Billings (Mont.) Gazette* reporter Lorna Thackeray, "It's not going to solve the riddle of Custer's last stand, but it may help us to put one or two of the pieces back together."

About Deep Ravine, Mangum told the Associated Press in mid-April that "We want to satisfy the question of were there any bodies down there, and if not, where did the missing soldiers fall and where are they buried."

That no one was certain what "the first inch-by-inch mapping of the entire battlefield" might reveal was evident from another Mangum comment: "We might surprise ourselves and find another skirmish line and shed more light on the battle. We want to find out exactly what evidence of the battle we have to possibly reconstruct more of it."

Scott, too, measured his words: "The application of historic archeological techniques to the study of the battle has the possibility of recovering and recording data which may aid in a better understanding of the events of the day."

Meanwhile, in April a Hardin, Mont., surveyor, Walt Egged, helped prepare the battlefield for what Court emphasized was actually "a survey," not a traditional archeological "dig." The 765-acre battlefield — 603 at the main grounds and 162 at Reno-Benteen — was divided into smaller 100-meter grid squares by Egged. Reference points at the grid intersections were staked out on the battlefield so that artifact loca-

Archeologist Richard Fox conducted his initial survey of the fire-blackened battlefield in August-September 1983.

(Dan Martinez)

tions could be "shot in" from a known geographical point. As a result, information about distances and bearings of artifacts could be fed into a computer in Lincoln, which would analyze the data and map the spatial distributions and relationships of the artifacts.

"That grid was invaluable," said Scott about Egged's professional survey. Using the grid system meant the precise location of every artifact could be preserved, even after it was removed from the ground. This information later was to be crucial in understanding battle events.

Elsewhere, the non-professional, the curious, the Custer buffs were getting ready as well.

THE 1984 DIG BEGINS

Story, Wyo., artist Ed Smyth, a slender man with the definitive Westerner's look about him, recalls how he first learned about the project: "Browsing through the spring issue of the *Custer Battlefield Dispatch*, I suddenly sat bolt upright, did a double take. Yep, there it was. 'Park receives green light for archeological dig.' Volunteers could be used. Wow!"

Smyth, who formerly worked in advertising copywriting for Ralston Purina in St. Louis, didn't hesitate to apply with "a silent prayer and high hopes." Smyth and "11 other recruits" who Scott called to take part in opening week were a odd assortment, including four senior citizens, a neurosurgeon, a lawyer, a computer specialist, a restaurant owner, and a bronc rider. "Men from all parts of the country," Smyth said.

The weather on the first day in the field, Tuesday May 8, was less than promising, as Smyth recalls: "The first morning was cold and blustery with spits of snow, but our chance of a lifetime was about to begin. Weather couldn't faze us."

Digging Into Custer's Last Stand

In May 1985, metal detecting crew members went through the tedious task of locating possible artifacts at the dump site on the Reno-Benteen field. The dump site would be the focus of attention four years later during the 1989 archeological dig.

(Sandy Barnard)

Perhaps the wittiest man participating in either the 1984 or 1985 digs, lawyer Murray Kloberdanz of Osage, Iowa, had driven to the battlefield through "spitting rain, sleet and snow" with his brother, Mike, a computer systems specialist from Cedar Rapids and a collector of Indian artifacts for more than 10 years.

In his 1984 journal Murray recalled their first day — Monday May 7 — when they rendezvoused in the Stone House below the national cemetery. The building, historic in its own right, was once the superintendent's quarters. "As I stood by the fireplace, I noticed three tiny holes in the mantel. I recalled my two brothers and I hanging our Christmas stockings in a like manner as did some superintendent's children in the past."

The next day the brothers joined the archeologists, Smyth and the other volunteers along the south battlefield fence to begin the metal detecting.

"Starting from the main road by a fence edging private land, we lined up," Smyth remembers. "Those with metal detectors spaced at 15-foot intervals, those without eyeballing the ground in between. As our almost military formation headed down the northeast slope toward Medicine Tail Coulee, the detectors began to sound off almost immediately."

Murray Kloberdanz has a slightly different recollection of that first move-out: "Four volunteers moved out approximately five yards apart to look for surface finds. Five volunteers, each equipped with metal detectors followed behind."

Scott says the first group moved without detectors, because he and Fox expected many surface finds. Also, true to their archeological roots, they didn't quite know what to do with metal detector operators and their hardware. "People have used just one or two or three detectors but they have not lined them up and used them as an inventory technique," he explained. "We honestly expected to see more artifacts on the surface because all the ground was burned off. You could see the surface."

He shook his head. "It still boggles my mind that after so many years modern artifacts from a battle so long ago are buried that deep."

To the surprise of pros and amateurs alike, the shrill chirp of the electronic detectors quickly became a symphony. Artifacts seemed to pour forth from the ground. "By the end of the first day it was clear as a bell that detectors was the way to do it," Scott said. With so much area to examine and with most objects buried beneath several inches of dirt, visual scanning of the surface wasn't going to work.

"So we shifted our emphasis," Scott said.

Back in Lincoln, one of Scott's friends, Dick Harmon, a contracting officer with the U.S. Geological Survey, was dying with envy. An expert on frontier firearms, Harmon stayed home that first week. "Doug hadn't expected much, so he talked me out of coming that first day," Harmon recalled. But Scott phoned Harmon that night to tell him of an exciting find — the back strap to a Colt pistol.

Harmon's response? An agonizing "Oh no!"

The artifact's value was not recognized immediately by those who found it, but a few moments of study convinced Scott of its importance. "That was an exciting moment," Scott recalled. "To realize we had a really important artifact of the battle the first day." The object's serial number later identified it as one issued to a Custer trooper.

Recording artifact finds on Last Stand Hill during the May 1984 dig.

(Dan Martinez)

Digging Into Custer's Last Stand

Metal detecting efforts proceeded meticulously to make certain artifacts would be recorded properly and not damaged or lost. An equipment buckle eventually surfaced at this Reno-Benteen site in May 1985. **(Sandy Barnard)**

That first day the "diggers" continued along the south fence to its junction with the eastern boundary. As volunteer Michael Parks of Everett, Wash., wrote later in *American West*, "Here just below Calhoun Hill, the detectors started singing wildly." Some 30 cartridges, most from Henry and Winchester repeating rifles, were recovered from the site, which became known as "Henryville."

Detecting methods weren't designed to locate every artifact on the field, just a sample that reflected accurately what was there. Also, archeologists traditionally leave something for later generations to find. To assure their sampling accuracy, the archeologists organized four crews for metal detecting. First, operators swept the field, keeping on line within each 100-meter grid. Each walked five meters, or 15 feet, from his neighbors. With each signal, a trailing volunteer marked the location with a small pin flag.

A recovery crew followed at a slower pace. Meticulously, they uncovered each object and an archeologist determined its probable historical value.

During the 1985 dig, Scott kidded that archeologists lack their own tools. They borrow trowels, pin flags, surveying instruments, paint brushes and picks from other occupations. But each served a purpose in locating or recording artifacts from the Battle of Little Bighorn.

The final crew were the recorders, who used a surveying instrument, or transit, to record, using the grid system, an object's precise battlefield location. Each item was tagged with a field number and secured in its own paper bag for later laboratory study.

Archeological Surveys at Custer Battlefield 1984-1985

Little incentive was needed on that first day to spur the volunteers, but an archeologist promised a case of beer to the first person who found a battle relic, Murray Kloberdanz recalled in a newspaper article. "I was on the far left of the line of the metal detectors and immediately got the sounding or 'hit' on my machine."

Alas, it proved to be a piece of modern wire.

"We moved approximately four feet when I received a second sounding: a sardine can of ancient vintage (because of the crude soldering). Doug examined it and said it was probably from the 1890s."

Nearby another volunteer, Stan Hart of Ellensburg, Wash., got a sounding and produced the first official find — a .45/55 cartridge of the type known to have been used by 7th Cavalry soldiers during the battle. Soon after, Murray discovered his own first artifact — a .52 caliber Spencer cartridge. "The excitement mounted as each member of the metal detecting team found rounds underground," he said.

In Henryville, other finds led to additional memorable moments. "I was also fortunate enough to find the first slug at the top of a small draw; again it was a .45/55," Kloberdanz said. "As we approached a small knoll, suddenly every member of the metal detecting team began to find .44 caliber Henry cartridges known to have been used by the Indians at the battle.

"In a crude line we found eight cartridges, all Henrys, approximately three to five feet apart. They all appeared to have been struck by the same firing pin and most likely were fired from the same weapon."

Englishman Derek Batten (center) waits patiently for fellow recording crew members Dick Harmon (left) and Pat Phillips (second from left) to finish data readings received from Doug Scott on top of the bluffs. In back of Don King, holding the stadia rod, is the Reno Retreat Crossing.

(Sandy Barnard)

A smashed slug, recovered in May 1984 on the main battlefield, tells its own story of one small part of the Battle of the Little Bighorn.
(Dan Martinez)

An incoming slug, unearthed at Reno-Benteen in May 1985, rests in the ground.
(Sandy Barnard)

Complete metal arrow point found at Last Stand Hill in May 1984.
(Dan Martinez)

Archeological Surveys at Custer Battlefield 1984-1985

As often happens at Custer Battlefield, imagination can present vivid pictures of what action must have been like on June 25, 1876. "I could see the Indian jumping up, shooting, ducking back down in the sage brush and moving three feet away in case the return fire from the soldiers was directed at his smoke. He would fire again and then move on until he expended all eight cartridges," Kloberdanz said.

Kloberdanz remembers a conversation that day with historian Mangum: "Neil stopped by and informed us that we had found more that Tuesday morning than had ever been recovered in the last 40 years!"

Old and new often intertwined. After lunch on day one, Kloberdanz found a .50/70 Indian slug between two beer cans in a trashy area on Calhoun Hill. Stan Hart received 11 soundings within a couple of feet of one another. All turned out to be 11 round nails of post-Custer vintage.

"Of course, we surmised that Stan initially deserved credit for finding where Custer's carpenter was shot! Stan vigorously denied the honor." Kloberdanz said.

Murray's final find of the day also proved of more recent vintage, certainly not of the Custer era — a modern marijuana pipe found in debris on Calhoun Hill. Other team members found modern debris, including .22 shells.

Ed Smyth recalled finding a kidney-shaped steel object, called a "strike-a-light," that was gripped in the fist and used for starting fires. When struck with flint, the striker would produce a shower of sparks. "Those rare pieces date back to Colonial times," he said.

Scott said the strike-a-light, probably lost during the fray, would have been obtained by the Indians from traders. Seventh Cavalry soldiers had phosphorus matches at the time of the battle. Part of a bridle was found buried under eight inches of soil.

"One of the boys found a beautiful gold-crested button," Smyth said. "He was ecstatic, until Doug Scott carefully turned it over and found it had an aluminum back! Some tourist had lost it from a blazer."

As luck would have, the same volunteer "turned up an honest-to-gosh uniform button," Smyth added. "These were very rare."

Murray Kloberdanz summed up Day One this way: "All in all, our historical finds made it quite a Tuesday!"

The metal detecting goal was to determine patterning — to let the artifacts' placement disclose the ebb and flow of the battle. As early as the second day, as the crew worked along the top of Calhoun Hill, artifacts were providing solid indications of new Indian and soldier positions and further insight into how the battle developed. Henryville was one of the new Indian positions.

"Within one-half hour we had over 40 flags to show for our efforts," Murray Kloberdanz said. "Mike and I happened to find a row of .45/55 cartridges showing where a skirmish line of soldiers had probably fired at the Indians. I also found a .44 Henry cartridge which had not been fired. Doug surmised that it was accidentally dropped by an Indian after the position was overrun."

The numerous artifacts found on Calhoun Hill above the area that had been dubbed Henryville clearly showed that Lt. Calhoun's troops had not fled in panic.

The fracture in this .45-.55 cartridge, found in May 1985 at Reno-Benteen, indicates it was fired in a larger caliber weapon, likely by an Indian.
(Sandy Barnard)

Merely junk? Actually, this piece was a cavalryman's cup recovered at Reno-Benteen in May 1985.
(Sandy Barnard)

Instead, the patterns of military cartridges indicated that organized resistance had taken place in that vicinity.

Although the project was still in its early stages, Scott and Fox were already realizing that their plans and schedule needed adjusting. For one thing visual reconnaissance now was secondary. Also, Scott said, "When we saw what was coming out of the ground, we determined it was going to be slow-going. Within the first week and a half I was convinced we would not get to Reno-Benteen. No question. There was going to have to be a second season."

Fox and he also realized that tighter organization would be needed in the future. That first year they had accepted nearly anyone willing to help, with a week's limit to allow more people to take part. But the lack of experience of the always willing volunteers actually slowed efforts often. At times, the slowdown was necessary to maintain the project's scientific accuracy.

"Maybe we expected too much of the volunteers. The amount of training we gave them probably was insufficient for what we were asking of them. The training we did give them took longer also. We also found it took a couple of days for people to get comfortable with their field procedures."

But the enthusiasm the volunteers brought with them both years compensated for their inexperience. "We did find that people got so involved that they hated to give it up and go home. Their interest was so consuming, which is wonderful, but they became so emotionally attached that they just didn't want to leave."

THE DIG CONTINUES

As the diggers moved on, surprisingly few artifacts were found between Calhoun Hill and the defensive position occupied by Company I, commanded by Captain Keogh on the east side of Battle Ridge. In the Keogh vicinity, the metal detecting instruments resumed their siren song.

"My brother Mike found a gold-colored button on the surface, a .36 caliber bullet in a draw and one rattlesnake skin," Murray Kloberdanz recalled. "To date we had encountered no rattlers but we were forewarned that they indeed were out there."

John Craig of Billings, Mont., found a horseshoe of 7th Cavalry origin. Murray Kloberdanz himself came across the first human remains to be located: a toe bone on the surface about three feet below a burial marker in a deep ravine near the Keogh area.

"We also found two different smashed Henry slugs in a cluster of markers. The archeologist determined that these slugs probably were the death slugs of those soldiers."

Soon after, Kloberdanz, working on the recovery team, came across a unique find — an unused, modern 13-cent stamp in a ravine. About this time, Ed Smyth found one of the oldest, although not battle-related, items. "There on a ridge lay a beautiful quartzite dart point for an atl-atl from the McKean complex, 3,500 to 5,000 years old. How it survived the fighting we'll never know, as there were shells and slugs all around it."

Thursday May 11 brought another noteworthy discovery for Murray Kloberdanz on the east side of Battle Ridge beyond the Keogh defensive area. "We continued sweeping toward a lone marker near the park boundary fence. As I neared the marker, my metal detector suddenly sounded. There, just beneath the surface, was an unfired Colt .45 pistol round.

"I imagined this desperate trooper running in his lone attempt to escape, feverishly fumbling to load his pistol to fend off the swarming Indians, dropping this shell which lay mute for 108 years as to his horrible fate on that Sunday afternoon."

Near Keogh's position a number of exciting artifacts were found, including a complete carbine sling snap hook (used by soldiers to secure their carbines by fastening a ring on their carbine stock to a sling on their body); the remains of a leather cavalry bridle; a horseshoe; a cavalry spur; slugs and casings from weapons fired by combatants on both sides.

Digging Into Custer's Last Stand

The bridle was found by Murray Kloberdanz and Marlin Howe, a retired electrician from Tipton, Iowa, while recovering an item in a nearby ravine. Pausing when they discovered leather two inches beneath the surface, they called Scott who diligently removed the bridle complete with a metal ring.

What would prove to be a major find of the season surfaced nearby also, when a metal detector sensed boot nails buried beneath the surface. The recovery crew located the remains of the actual boot, its top sliced off by the Indians to use the leather in pouches. Scott and Fox decided the site merited further attention since human toe bones and a cervical vertebra had also been found nearby. The latter had been discovered jutting out of the soil by Mike Kloberdanz. Next to it was a soldier's suspender button.

During the second week an excavation block — a 2 x 2 meter square — was sunk at that point and yielded, just inches from the boot, still more fascinating materials, including bones from a human forearm and a lower leg, complete with foot and toe bones.

Soon opening week drew to a close, and the Kloberdanz brothers headed home, richer by $50 apiece. Volunteers, in the first year only, received $10 per day subsistence from the Custer Battlefield Historical & Museum Association. But the experience meant more to the brothers, and would draw them back in 1985. "As Mike and I drove across the Dakota plains, we reflected on our experiences during the week at Custer Battlefield: we learned much about the battle, we had made new friends and we had helped contribute to the knowledge of this violent clash of cultures," Murray said in summing up their week.

The Kloberdanz brothers weren't the only ones enthusiastic about the project. Jim Court found himself spending more and more time shepherding media representatives around the battlefield. "The excitement out here is really catching," he told Associated Press on Friday May 11. Camera crews from the major television networks were expected the next week.

How meaningful was the experience for other volunteers? Reporter Lorna Thackeray of the *Billings Gazette* quoted several in a wrap-up article on Sunday May 13.

• Retired neurosurgeon Jess T. "Doc" Schwidde of Billings: "One of my biggest thrills since being here is finding a Henry cartridge fired by an Indian. It's a thrill to think that it will be in a museum someday."

• John Craig, also of Billings, explained why he was keeping a journal of his experience: "It will be something to show my grandchildren some day."

• Marlin Howe: "It's one of the greatest experiences I've ever had in my life. It's fun, it really is."

• Ed Rosco of Billings, who spent a day of volunteer service: "I was really impressed with the area — all the sorrow and suffering was all laid out."

MORE SURPRISES IN 1984

As the 1984 field season progressed, more and more surprises popped up. For example, during Week 3 metal detectors located fragile steel arrowheads.

Archeological Surveys at Custer Battlefield 1984-1985

Newspaper headlines seemed to trumpet the obvious — "Bows used in Custer fight, study proves." But even routine discoveries carried historical meaning. "We always assumed that most of the Indians had bows and arrows," Court explained to reporters. "But arrowheads were very thin, and rusted easily and disintegrated over the years."

The researchers understood how valuable bows and arrows were to Indians fighting in rolling, grassy hills around Battle Ridge. Staying out of sight of the troopers' long-range Springfield carbines, warriors lofted their arrows into military positions with deadly efficiency.

As more and more shell casings and slugs were uncovered, the archeologists realized another reason, besides disintegration, accounted for the lack of arrow heads: The Indians had been well-armed with a variety of firearms, more so than perhaps had been believed before the dig.

Besides cartridges, more goodies surfaced including an 1870 5-cent piece. In addition, evidence of a previously unknown Indian position was found not more than 20 feet from the front of the present-day Visitor's Center.

Of greater significance were finds along what has been called, somewhat controversially, the South Skirmish Line. In 1985, visitors knew the line of markers as the Deep Ravine Trail without realizing the controversy over whether it marked an area of ferocious fighting, or where panicky soldiers fleeing Custer Hill met their demise. However, artifacts along this sloping area below Custer Hill provided bountiful evidence that the soldiers waged a ferocious defense here. Detecting crews uncovered hundreds of shells, scored slugs, tunic buttons and other evidence of a fight.

Several excavations were sunk at markers along the trail, and most revealed bone materials and evidence of the determined defense. The most startling find — a human finger bone, still encircled by a wedding band. Court termed the finger bone, uncovered about two inches below the ground about 200 yards from the Visitor's Center, "as the biggest find of the year so far." Although it probably had little scientific value, Court added that "It's the most personal item found so far."

At the very least, Rich Fox suggested, "It's exciting from a layman's point of view."

Montanans Vernel Wagner, an artist from Big Timber, and Dean Kenney, a veteran metal detector operator from Billings, gained credit for the find. "By golly, I thought it was a bullet," Kenney said. "It had the reading of a bullet."

Wagner said, "I wanted to find something really important. It's going to take me a week to get over this one."

In the field, speculation abounded that the inch-long, light brown finger bone had been severed, perhaps by a trophy-seeking warrior. However, post-project study of the bone by forensic anthropologist Clyde Snow ruled out that theory.

As the June 7 closing date for 1984 neared, Scott, Fox and Court were amazed at what had been retrieved during the five weeks. The artifact total exceeded 1,800, and more than 1,100 ultimately would prove to be battle-related.

The harvest actually had a negative side. The Reno-Benteen Defense Site, also scheduled for inventorying, clearly had to await another year. Also, more money

Digging Into Custer's Last Stand

— Court estimated $10,000 to $20,000 — would be necessary for lab study in Lincoln, Neb., at the Midwest Archeological Center.

Lab tests weren't necessary for Scott to conclude one important fact about the Battle of Little Bighorn: "Custer and his men were not only outnumbered by the Indians. They were also outgunned."

PREPARING FOR YEAR NO. 2

Realizing a second year in the field was necessary, Scott and Fox confronted two tasks in late summer 1984: Writing their reports about Year No. 1 and preparing for Year No. 2. The Reno-Benteen Defense Site had not been inventoried, and more marble markers on the Custer field needed to be excavated to guarantee the validity of sampling techniques.

Also, the major puzzle of Deep Ravine remained as mysterious as ever. Despite extensive metal detecting, the use of power augers to drill holes in promising areas, and excavations of several mound sites, no sign of Company E had materialized. That failure encouraged some Custer buffs to retain their convictions that the geological feature long labeled as Deep Ravine was historically inaccurate.

Both archeologists believed the ravine still deserved serious study of its soil strata by a geomorphological expert. Interested in participating was Vance Haynes, a University of Arizona expert with a world-wide reputation, who also is a leading authority on the Springfield carbine.

Before planning the second campaign, they, first, needed more money from the Custer Battlefield Historical & Museum Association for lab study of 1984's artifacts. In early October the association approved some $6,000 for that task and another $10,000 for the 1985 dig (By early 1986, the association had provided $42,998 for the two projects and the original survey by Rich Fox, Business Manager Shirley Coates said).

The association was just as eager to see the project continue, after a record year of financial growth through dues collected from its 1,200 members and sales at its bookstore in the battlefield's Visitors Center. At the fall annual meeting, Coates reported revenues had about doubled that year.

Also, the archeological project's national and regional publicity had led to a 16 percent increase in visitors, Court reported, and record throngs had come in May and early June. Media attention had been staggering. The three major television networks carried stories and several major magazines planned articles, including *Life* and *American History Illustrated*. *Time* magazine had carried a late May account of the dig, and the *Bismarck (N. D.) Tribune*, whose correspondent Mark Kellogg died with Custer, sent a two-person reporter-photographer team.

Across the West local newspapers had carried stories, and Associated Press and United Press International provided accounts to their members. TV stations from Spokane, Wash., Salt Lake City, Utah, Rapid City, S. D., Denver, Colo., and Billings, Missoula and Hardin, Mont., had all covered the story.

Scott and Court considered the dig's media coverage a mixed blessing. In one article Scott said media attention "cost Rich and me a little time in the field, probably a couple of days, because we're not used to working on that basis. But it's also part of the job. It's a public site and a public job, and people have a right to know what their money's being used for."

Court said that many days Mangum and he spent more time with news media than on battlefield duties. "We just didn't expect to get this much publicity."

Media errors did haunt the archeologists, but none more so than an Associated Press account of a Boston speech Scott gave in early January 1985 outlining his findings to the Society of Historical Archeology. AP reported that "During the dig 117 individual Indian weapons were found."

Scott shakes his head wistfully, noting that in two years of work not a single weapon was uncovered. However, the post-dig study of the 1984 cartridges indicated the Indians fired at least 117 individual weapons on June 25, 1876. "I think everyone who participated would have liked to have found an actual weapon," Scott said. "We just had to be satisfied with the evidence that indicated they fired at least 117 different weapons."

Early in 1986, Scott said the enormous continuing interest in the project surprised him. "Most archeological projects generate some local media interest in the actual project area. Stories may be done, but once it ends, interest subsides."

But the Custer project continues generating inquiries. "I guess even with the news media it surprises me how Custer's name can evoke so much emotion and still be a great story after 110 years. Many archeological projects are more revealing about our past human behavior and the study of past cultures, but this project dominates the public's interest."

Why the continuing allure? "From my personal standpoint, having been on the battlefield, knowing those marble markers evoke an image ... you can see patterns, whole groups of them. It makes it very intriguing. I think if the battlefield were just a patch of ground with no markers, things might be different."

But, he adds, you can't overlook the "Custer mystique. He was a hero at his death and he did die there. And the mystery about what happened continues until today."

PRODUCING NEW INFORMATION ABOUT THE CUSTER BATTLE

Lab analysis may be less exciting for TV crews seeking exciting video, but behind-the-scenes work during the winter of 1984-1985 underscored the project's value and the validity of its techniques. Gradually, as each item was studied, the archeologists realized a vast data base of battle information was being created.

Contributing to this was an IBM Fastdraft computer graphics system used through the courtesy of Southeast Community College in Milford, Neb., which shared its facilities with them. Identifications and grid coordinates of some 1,800 items were color coded appropriately for the computer — blue for cavalry and red for Indian. Data included ballistics information from cartridge tests conducted by the Nebraska State Highway Patrol Ballistics Laboratory and from forensic studies on bones by Dr. Clyde C. Snow in Norman, Okla.

The Fastdraft program permits the displaying of a battlefield map on the computer screen. An attached pen plotter can reproduce a paper copy of what amounts to a flow chart of the battle which is stunning in its implications. It details the trail of marked cartridges and other artifacts in patterns that suggest how soldiers fought and fell. Individual movements can be traced literally as shells and cartridges from individual weapons are plotted first at one point, then another, finally a third.

When a weapon is fired, its firing pin and extractor leave signatures, or indentations, that are as individualistic as a human's fingerprints. Lab personnel can pinpoint which recovered cartridges were fired by the same weapon. With such information, they can document how a single firearm was carried about and used at more than one location on the battlefield. Coupled with precise knowledge of where the cartridges themselves were found, this information enables researchers to trace individual firearms, if not their actual bearers, about the field, and can give insight into the flow of events on June 25. In addition, such ballistics information helps researchers to identify types of weapons used and to determine an approximate number of each type that might have been involved in the Little Bighorn fight.

Turning Custer history upside down was not the archeologists' purpose, Scott maintains, but the new information certainly calls for further study by students of the Battle of Little Bighorn. "It is possible to trace an individual's movements on the battlefield, or at least the movement of an individual weapon," Scott said. "We can clearly see Indian positions that we weren't aware of previously, and we can clearly demonstrate that they were armed with a much greater number and variety of firearms than people thought, including a large number of lever-action Winchester rifles. At that time, they were state of the art."

Based on the evidence of the 117 weapons in use during the battle against the soldiers, Scott and Fox believe the Indians had perhaps three times as many, or 350 firearms, and perhaps many more. They also believe that, based on six positions the team located where Indians took cover and surrounded Custer's men, that no Errol Flynn-style battle took place. Instead, the Indians fought cautiously, seldom showing themselves, content to pick off soldiers a few at a time. Once the dismounted cavalry ranks were thinned, a final swarming overran whoever remained.

"It certainly goes against the popular myth" of Indians on ponies circling the soldiers, Scott said, although the flow of battle action strongly suggests a "last stand" likely did occur at Custer's position.

The first year's dig also offered convincing proof that the soldiers had held their ground wherever they fought. Only sheer overwhelming odds, not battle panic, led to their defeat. "My feeling is, based on the artifact pattern, that the men must have fairly well held their positions."

A New Look For 1985

In preparing for Year 2, Scott, Fox and Court decided on some organizational changes. For one thing, they wanted to make better use of the skills of individual volunteers. "During the first year we learned that we should ask more what people wanted to do rather than merely assign them to tasks," Scott said.

Also, they invited only people who had either experience or special skills, not just any Custer buff who wandered in. In addition, they asked each for at least a two-week commitment. Between 200 and 300 people applied, but Scott chose only about 60 to participate. The largest group offered metal detecting experience, as the inventory of the Reno-Benteen site would be more difficult because of its rougher terrain and heavier growth, especially sage brush. Located four miles from the Custer field, Reno-Benteen had not been burned over in 1983.

The first year the two archeologists had been impressed with the metal detecting expertise of two veteran users, Irwin and Riva Lee of Turlock, Calif. So Scott asked Irwin, who represents the Fisher Company in 11 western states, to serve as detector adviser for the entire second dig, which would run between May 6 and June 7. Along with this writer, the Lees were the only volunteers to spend that entire period at the battlefield.

Irwin's a heavy-set fellow who fits the part of a top sergeant well, and that's exactly the way he ran his metal detecting crews in the field. No nonsense. Everyone expected to do his part. He took on the task not only out of historical interest but also to improve relations between metal detecting enthusiasts and professionals in archeology. Usually the two sides mix with the peacefulness of gasoline and fire.

Riva, whom everyone considered the mother hen of the crew, had a more simple explanation for their involvement: "We just like to find good things in the ground."

As the archeologists and the first group of volunteers gathered on Sunday May 5, expectations ran even higher than on the initial week-end in 1984. Court and the two archeologists were certain more artifacts would be found in the five weeks within the 162 acres controlled by the NPS at Reno-Benteen.

"We'll probably be seeing different kinds of artifacts at the Reno-Benteen site," Court said. Mangum commented, "That is where the pack train was. And they were there for two days instead of just a few hours. The potential for finding more complete skeletal remains is very good there."

Scott agreed, noting that in 1958 a limited archeological project had un-covered remains of several soldiers at Reno-Benteen. Scott also enlisted three specialists to participate on site during the dig. During the second week forensic anthropologist Snow, who had examined the first year's bone materials, planned to spend five days at the battlefield. Starting in the fourth week, geomorphologist Haynes would spend 10 days scouring Deep Ravine and the surrounding countryside looking for geological clues to unlock the mystery of the missing Company E.

The third specialist was Dick Harmon, a contracting officer on special assignment from the U.S. Geological Survey to assist the archeologists. An expert in period firearms, he would help identify bullets, cartridges or weapons retrieved during the study. Harmon proved to be the project's utility man, able to operate the transit, scrape away dirt from an artifact, or act as a mule to carry equipment to an excavation site. Probably no one worked harder than Dick Harmon.

Once again for 1985, Scott, by virtue of his NPS position, held administrative responsibility for the dig. Actual field leadership was divided three ways: Scott would supervise the metal detection inventory of the Reno-Benteen battlefield; Fox would direct Deep Ravine work again; and Melissa Connor, who had participated for several weeks in 1984, would be crew chief from the outset, overseeing

Digging Into Custer's Last Stand

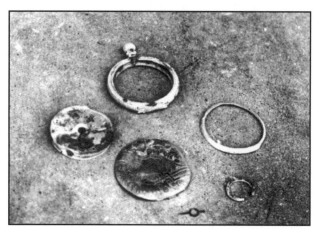

Among the more intriguing artifacts recovered by metal detecting crews during either dig was this collection of six pieces of a pocket watch, found in the Reno-Benteen hospital area in May 1985.

(Sandy Barnard)

excavations planned for 18 marble markers on the main battlefield. Fox and Connor, a senior research archeologist with the University of Nebraska, Lincoln, actually were hired under a co-operative agreement with Nebraska.

In addition, Jim Court had asked me to advise the archeologists and the park service personnel on media relations.

All was ready for Year No. 2. Still, Scott took a cautious attitude about what could be accomplished. "We aren't changing history, and we aren't dispelling the myths about Custer," the Associated Press quoted him a few days before the dig. Despite his caution, a potential time bomb was ticking behind the scenes that would threaten to scuttle the project in its second week.

A STUMBLING START IN 85

The spits of snow from 1984 were absent on Monday May 6, the first morning of 1985's project. Crisp weather but plenty of sunshine greeted the first 20 volunteers, who squeezed into two adjoining first floor rooms of the Stone House for a briefing from the three project archeologists and Jim Court.

A subdued Scott had to tell them that field work would be delayed until at least Wednesday. That's when officials from the Montana State Historic Preservation Office and the Advisory Council on Historical Preservation would meet with the archeologists to hear first-hand what Scott and company intended to carry out at Custer Battlefield that year. At issue was compliance with the Historic Preservation Act, which requires persons undertaking archeological or other significant activity affecting an historic site such as the battlefield (listed on the National Register of Historic Places) to justify their plans. The act, originally intended to protect historic sites from "adverse effects" of construction, also covers research projects.

No clearance had been sought, either for 1985 or for 1984, because both years Court and the archeologists, whose work proposals had been reviewed by the NPS Denver Regional Office, figured their projects would have no "adverse effect" and did not require extensive consultations. But at the last minute, officials, in particular those at the Montana state level who were unhappy that their review had not been sought beforehand, interpreted matters differently, and that forced Scott to admit to those in the Stone House that "We (NPS) were wrong." However, he was optimistic that clearance would come, perhaps at Wednesday's meeting.

So opening day gloom subsided as other activities were substituted: briefings and a tour of the entire battlefield by Historian Mangum. Tuesday would be devoted to checking equipment and field procedures at Reno-Benteen, but no formal collection of artifacts was sanctioned.

The volunteers took the delay in good stride, although several noted the irony of the project's dilemma compared to what was happening just outside the nationally protected grounds. A road-widening project for U.S. Highway 212 had sheared through hillocks and swales close to Last Stand Hill that undoubtedly had been involved in the Custer fight. Apparently, no one had considered the probable adverse effects of that construction project.

Metal detector operator Bob Johnson of Hersey, Mich., expressed a wistful desire, shared no doubt by the other detector operators, to test dirt shoved aside by road equipment. Scott and Court understood their feelings, but ruled that under the circumstances no one should operate a metal detector anywhere near the battlefield until approval was received.

Alas, Wednesday's meeting produced no permission to start work. Court and the archeological team explained their goals and outlined their plans to limit any battlefield damage. While officials seemed sensitive to the constraints of time — time for archeologists and time for volunteers — none could utter the magic word, "Begin." Instead, they had to consult with their superiors in the state capital at Helena and at the NPS Regional Office in Denver.

Court and the archeologists, although frustrated, tried to be upbeat. Court hoped NPS Regional Director Lorraine Mintzmyer would authorize the dig before a technically required signature of the Advisory Council president was obtained. But Court cautioned reporters that "a slight possibility" existed that the entire effort might have to be abandoned.

Volunteers grumbled about petty bureaucratic politics at the state and federal level. But they willingly pitched in to help the park service map fence lines and tombstone markers, something that hadn't been done since the 1890s. That effort would prove revealing before the field work ended. When the team finished mapping marker positions, they discovered only 242 sites existed, not the 260 or so talked about for so many years.

Just when it appeared that boredom might win the battle of the volunteers' first week, word came that inventorying at Reno-Benteen could begin but Connor could not undertake excavations at markers yet. Formal approval for that was expected the following week. So in the meantime the professionals and volunteers threw themselves into their metal detecting.

As Lorna Thackeray reported in the Friday May 10 *Billings Gazette*, "Metal detectors beeped a happy chorus over Custer Battlefield National Monument Thursday (May 9) as word arrived from Denver that archeologists could begin digging."

By day's end some 200 artifacts had been recovered from an area just inside the Reno-Benteen main gate on the east side of the battlefield road below Sharpshooter's Ridge. As expected, most finds were bullets and cartridges from Indian and cavalry weapons. Gaining the nod as the year's first exciting artifact was a circular piece of metal that had almost been overlooked as junk. It looked like a metal washer with a hole in its center. However, Dick Harmon recognized the object as actually the back of an eye piece to a metal telescope. It was found along the presumed route Reno and Benteen's troops followed in their slow move to Weir Point and their subsequent retreat.

Several finds were made at the point where Sharpshooter's Ridge overlooks the Reno-Benteen defense perimeter. The story of how an Indian with a Sharp's rifle sent bullet after bullet toward the soldiers, picking off several men, was uppermost in the crew members' minds as they moved through the area.

The news media, headed by the first of three crews representing Cable News Network, turned out to pick up the story from 1984. The focus often fell on the volunteers themselves.

For example, Craig Repass, who along with his wife Lois was among the hardest working and best-liked of the participants, talked about his book, *Custer For President*, which grew out of his master's thesis at North Carolina State University. He debunks the theory that Custer launched an ill-advised attack on the Indians hoping to gain the Democratic presidential nomination. "There is no concrete proof that he ever considered running in 1876," Repass, a Georgia resident, said.

At a lunch break, Val Gass, a retired railroader from Salt Lake City, sat on the bluffs overlooking the Reno retreat route from the valley and enthusiastically answered a Billings TV reporter's questions. When she asked if he ever were tempted to steal artifacts, he looked at her incredulously. "Heavens no, that's a part of history and it's exciting just to see these items coming out of the ground after 109 years."

Gass, who himself survived a legendary U.S. military encounter as a crew member on the USS Arizona on the day Japan bombed Pearl Harbor, added that it's more important for artifacts to be studied so future generations can have the information.

Other volunteers caught the media's attention. Brian Pohanka, a writer-researcher for Time-Life Books in Alexandria, Va., impressed one South Dakota TV reporter, with his awesome grasp of the historical record surrounding the Custer story. Wearing a distinctive pit helmet, Milo McLeod, an archeologist for the National Forest Service stationed at Lolo National Forest near Missoula, represented the Montana National Guard.

Roye Lindsay, park superintendent at Fort Hartsuff in Nebraska, harbored no doubts about finding the 28 men of Company E in Deep Ravine. He had a pair of long, specially built slender rods, with a ball-bearing on one end, which could be shoved into the ground to detect bone materials close to the surface. His failure to hit anything did not diminish his enthusiasm for the project, which he called "a well-organized, unique approach to historical archeology."

One writer changed roles. Joe Stevens of Chicago told officials he planned to do free-lance articles about the dig. Given an orange road worker's plastic vest to mark him, along with the volunteers, as authorized to be working on the battlefield, and free rein to mingle with the crew, he soon was among the metal detecting crew uncovering artifacts.

Archeological Surveys at Custer Battlefield 1984-1985

"This is a 'Custerphile's' dream," he told the *Billings Gazette*, spilling his true motivations for coming west.

By the end of a shorter week than anticipated, Scott was pleased by the number of objects recovered — about 350 — and the variety, including an Indian bracelet, an Army tin cup and scores of cartridges. "The range of artifacts is still pretty much what we expected," he explained.

The second week would be more difficult for the crews, he added. "We will be moving onto the bluffs above the river and start working those areas. They will take a little longer than the rest of the Reno-Benteen area which is pretty flat."

Reno-Benteen also would take longer because, just as in 1984, many more artifacts were still in the ground, although that wasn't surprising, given the different circumstances between the two battle grounds. Custer's subordinates had many more men — about 350 — and had fought for two days, not two hours. "There were 350 men in the defense perimeter itself and they probably dropped a lot of stuff," Scott said.

THE SECOND BATTLE OF LITTLE BIGHORN

Volunteer workers dubbed it the Second Battle of Little Bighorn. One suggested it was "Custer's revenge."

Brian Pohanka suggested, "If it was any other battlefield, this couldn't have been pulled off."

What was pulled off? An amazing display of citizens' action at the grass roots, carried out by some 30 volunteers assisting the 1985 archeological survey. Amid great enthusiasm on the second Monday — May 13 — they had hit the field, the stop-and-go of Week 1 seemingly behind them. Because expectations were so high, or because the volunteers had little grasp of the nature of bureaucracies, they were unprepared, as everyone gathered on the front lawn of the Stone House, for what they were about to hear at noon Tuesday May 14 from Jim Court and Doug Scott.

Shortly before noon that day, about the time Fox, Connor and the volunteers were heading in from Reno-Benteen for the lunch break, Scott and Court had learned that NPS Regional Director Mintzmyer had decreed that the Custer Battlefield Archeological Survey must cease until it complied fully with the 1979 Historic Preservation Act — at least a four to six-week process. Officially, activity was merely being "deferred" until at least July 1, when full compliance probably could be obtained.

The decision was stunning. Scott and Court understood "deferred" actually meant, because of circumstances, "canceled." The archeologists had other summer commitments, and by June Court would need the quarters temporarily housing volunteers for NPS seasonal staffers. Also, many volunteers had taken vacation time, making their return later that summer unlikely. The unpaid volunteers, drawn from across the country, were irate at the prospect of heading home early. More important, they sincerely believed in the project and saw no need to wait.

"Adverse impact, indeed," one volunteer muttered. "We're the last ones to ransack this place."

Digging Into Custer's Last Stand

Pohanka, probably the most outspoken, termed the situation "unfair. They have no regard for history. This is a sham. Petty bureaucrats playing red tape games."

But as much as he empathized with the volunteers, Scott said later, "I thought it was over for 1985." He and the other archeologists had been ordered to return by Friday to Lincoln.

However, a fire storm of protest was building that Fox later would call "one of the most amazing things in my life." He added, "The project got canceled about noon on that Tuesday and 48 hours later we got orders — orders, not a request — from the Interior secretary's office to go back to work."

Never underestimate the power of citizens' action!

Scott and Court, because of their positions, could not urge anything but compliance with the Mintzmyer edict. Instead, the volunteers launched their own "last stand." Colleen Winchell of Billings, Mont., and Phil Frey of Bozeman, Mont., immediately organized an ad hoc Project Crisis Committee to call congressmen or anyone else who could help.

Pohanka and I began contacting the news media. By late Tuesday afternoon, both major wire services, the four major television news networks, the *Washington Post* and other major newspapers, and numerous regional newspapers and television and radio stations had been advised about the cancellation and the volunteers' efforts to reverse the decision.

One suggestion died quickly — carry placards of protest around the monument atop Last Stand Hill, a short distance from the spot where tradition says Custer fell. Instead, a placard of another sort — the telephone — became the instrument of protest.

Don Heffernan, W. Allis, Wis., called Sen. William Proxmire of his state. Buck Newbury, Burwell, Neb., contacted Sen. James Exxon of Nebraska. Frey phoned Montana Gov. Ted Schwinden.

Several Montanans contacted Eastern District Congressman Ron Marlenee, whose aid would prove crucial in the 48-hour effort. Marlenee's district includes the Custer Battlefield and he is a ranking member of the House Interior Committee, which oversees the Department of Interior and the National Park Service.

Bob Johnson called his Michigan representative Bill Schutte. Ed Smyth contacted Wyoming Gov. Ed Herschler and the state's senators, Malcolm Wallop and Allen Simpson. John Husk, Englewood, Colo., called his senators, Gary Hart and Bill Armstrong, plus three congressmen. On their second dig, Mike and Murray Kloberdanz called their Iowa congressional representatives. An interesting cross-breeding of contacts occurred when Bismarck, N. D., TV reporter Darrell Dorgan, at the battlefield to cover the dig, called his brother, Congressman Byron Dorgan. All in all, help was sought from at least 16 senators or congressmen.

Many volunteers tried other channels. Irwin Lee called his boss at the Fisher Company in California. Another detector operator, Lucy Bowen of Spokane, Wash., contacted the president of Garrett Electronics in Texas. Members of the Little Big Horn Associates, Custer Battlefield Historical & Museum Association, and Order of the Indian Wars were contacted by volunteers.

As the afternoon wore on, people sought other means to express their outrage. Winchell and I drafted a telegram of protest that was sent to President Ronald Reagan, who had played Custer in one of his movies, "Santa Fe Trail." The telegram, signed by 31 volunteers, cost $41.30. It read:

"I wish to protest the cancellation of the 1985 Archeological Survey of the Custer Battlefield National Monument by the Denver office of the National Park Service. As a volunteer working with the project, I feel strongly that the project is of great historical value and should be allowed to continue. Continued delay will cause the loss of professional archeological staff and civilian volunteers, in effect terminating the project."

No one added up how much the countless individual long-distance telephone calls cost. One quip: "AT&T is behind the cancellation. They're the only ones profiting from it."

By 5 p. m., Montana time, Project Crisis had slowed its campaign. Washington offices had closed two hours before and those in the mountain time zone were ending their day. That night a regular weekly outdoor barbecue was held, amid great uncertainty. Hope persisted, but was there enough time to turn the situation around? By morning positive signals were filtering back from Denver and Washington, D.C., indicating the media-congressional blitz was having an effect. Various agencies were looking for face-saving ways to put the volunteers back behind their metal detectors and trowels.

Early Thursday the go-ahead came for the project to resume immediately. A few details concerning marker excavations needed ironing out, but Project Crisis had succeeded. An aide to Montana Rep. Ron Marlenee relayed the positive, although somewhat puzzling, word: "NPS has agreed that tomorrow (Friday May 16) digging can start on Deep Ravine only."

"Digging" wasn't scheduled for Deep Ravine until later after Vance Haynes arrived. One wag suggested: "They're hoping we'll disappear down there like Company E and never be heard from again!"

Scott related how one official told him that "It's interesting that 30 people can have that much power." Denver NPS spokesman Jim Harpster told the *Denver Post* on Saturday May 18, "There is no question about it. The popular response has been widespread and continuous. There is no exaggerating the degree of interest in this activity."

Many volunteers chuckled at the remark, responding with "I told you so" remarks. Colorado's John Husk said, "Obviously somebody over-calculated or miscalculated on this situation and is now looking for a place to hide."

A final irony: By week's end, about 75 percent of the original volunteers who had won the Second Battle of Little Bighorn had headed home, their two-week stints having expired. That weekend, newcomers arrived to replace them behind the metal detectors and in the excavation pits.

Postscript: In early June, Mary Lou Grier, NPS deputy director, responding for Reagan to the volunteers' telegram, noted the cancellation had been ordered because the park service failed to send compliance forms to the Montana State Historic Preservation Officer as required by law.

Digging Into Custer's Last Stand

"But, in view of the significance of the survey and the all-important contributions of the volunteers, the mandated compliance forms were processed and ... the compliance procedure was thus expedited...."

She added, "We will be following the progress of the survey now scheduled to run through June 7. Such an undertaking, supported by large numbers of volunteers working under the supervision of Park Service professionals to enhance our knowledge of a significant event in our common heritage, is a vital element of President Reagan's 'New Federalism'."

A NEW BEGINNING

On Monday May 20, a new spirit prevailed. No longer did the shadow of cancellation hover over the project. Because of the field time that had been lost, the archeologists were anxious to focus on the dig. But the next few weeks wouldn't be easy for two reasons. Rising temperatures would reach 90 or higher in the hot sun on the wind-swept bluffs of Reno-Benteen.

Problem No. 2 would be the rugged bluffs themselves which sweep from the parking lot like wrinkled fingers reaching to the river below. Volunteers, lugging heavy equipment, gained an appreciation for what Reno's panic-stricken men faced after the Indians forced them to flee for their lives from the valley up these bluffs. The soil itself has a sandy texture, and is loose under foot. One afternoon I found myself skiing down a slope, which slipped away under foot. As I thudded to a stop in a swale between two high bluff lines, I found grass as green as back home in Indiana. Water rushing off the bluffs slips through the swales to the Little Bighorn River a few hundred feet west.

The week's artifact hunt began in the defense perimeter itself with the hollow swale south of today's parking lot as a focal point. Wide-open on its east end and vulnerable to gun fire from the Indians, the site had shielded horses and mules, which were picketed at the open end, and a make-shift hospital for the wounded men. The swale yielded a treasure trove of artifacts. In one place, about two inches below ground, a detector operator located a 12-inch iron picket pin, still standing straight after 109 years in the place where horses or mules had been tied to it. Not far away, Riva Lee pinpointed an engraved back of a gold-plated hunting case pocket watch. Later, five more pieces would be found. Working mole-like, Ron Nichols, an aerospace engineer from Costa Mesa, Calif., spent an hour digging out a horseshoe buried about a foot below the ground near the upper end of the swale.

On Wednesday May 22 Terry Osborn, Billings, Mont., and John Husk of Colorado claimed a record find of 13 shells and bullets in one "glory" hole. During Week 2, Murray Kloberdanz had discovered a hole that yielded seven shells. Osborn and Husk not only nearly doubled his total, they also found two fully loaded .45/55 cartridges. More significantly, the archeologists believe the site is a previously unknown entrenchment that should undergo more traditional archeological investigation in the future.

On Tuesday May 21, the crew recovered a one-day record of 373 artifacts. That also pushed the artifacts' total past 1,300, with at least 85 percent likely battle-related.

Unfortunately, to make up for lost time in the field, Scott had to postpone formal cleaning, study and entry of data about artifacts into the computer until everything was moved to Lincoln after the dig.

"It's more important to find the artifacts," Scott explained. "We are recording where each is found so we will have it for the lab work later."

Just as the year before, he and the other professionals were being pleasantly surprised by the variety of what the battlefield was yielding — cuff and collar buttons, various types of knives, spurs, horseshoes, a carbine socket for holding a carbine sling, and a brass plate from a saddle.

The watch parts fascinated crew members, especially Riva Lee, who one day had to be almost literally dragged away from Reno-Benteen. Earlier discoveries had come within a few yards of each other, and she was determined to find more. Markings on the watch suggested it was Swiss-made. At least a dozen 7th Cavalrymen were Swiss-born, raising intense speculation. On the inner workings letters "M" and "W" appeared to be engraved. Quipsters suggested the watch had belonged to Montgomery Ward. It was later identified as a period watch made in Switzerland as an inexpensive import, Scott said.

As one of the three major tasks for 1985, inventorying at Reno-Benteen was a success. By the end of the five weeks, more than 3,100 artifacts would be retrieved, and the majority were bullets and shells from Reno-Benteen, indicating, just as in 1984, the Indians were well-armed.

While all of Reno-Benteen was searched, archeologists believe more work remains there. Late in the dig, detector operators found themselves overwhelmed with hits just below the bluffs. The area soon overflowed with multi-colored pin flags. Scott had the detecting group, which included Tom Switajewski, a Navy man from Hanford, Calif., and Dean Kenney, Billings, collect a random sample of artifacts. The rest would remain until another time when traditional archeological dig methods could recover what appeared to be the dump site for the Reno-Benteen force.

History records that when the Reno-Benteen cavalrymen moved off the site after they were relieved on June 27 by the Terry-Gibbon column, they left behind considerable debris, including broken equipment, pack saddles and tack boxes. The troops burned the items to make them useless to scavenging Indians. The digging crew in 1985 found nails and other metal objects that appeared to have been in a fire. Scott labeled the site "a significant find," but was concerned that vandals might loot it. Thus, the exact location was not publicly disclosed.

THE HUMAN REMAINS

Two 1985 volunteers may have been more frustrated than the archeologists when red tape delayed the marker excavations. Clyde Snow had arrived Saturday May 11 to spend several days reviewing bone materials in the museum and any new 1985 field discoveries.

Writer-researcher Brian Pohanka is considered by many as a leading authority on the life of Capt. Myles Keogh, who died commanding Company I. In 1982, his research led battlefield officials to move the marble marker designating where Keogh had fallen. In 1985, Pohanka was anxious to see what might be found at the relocated marker.

Unfortunately, both men had to leave before excavations could begin, and they missed the excitement that soon followed. At Keogh's marker, for example, on Wednesday May 22 volunteer archeologists Rich Fike of the Utah Bureau of Land Management and Colleen Winchell, Billings, uncovered a rib bone, other bone fragments and part of a wooden stake that may have been an original grave marker. Court told reporters, "It's good to know the historic record corresponds with the archeological fact."

At another site, uphill from Keogh's, crew members found two wrist bones, a finger bone and part of a vertebra. At both markers, cobblestones that likely came from the Little Bighorn River were uncovered, also. The finds may seem small, but archeologist Connor stressed that the simplest items — from scraps of bones to buttons of underwear — could confirm whether a marker was an historically accurate death or burial site. "Parts is parts," all the professionals agreed.

Snow said that in his experience police today seldom recover all parts of a body exposed to the elements for any period. "They don't know what they are looking for, and are content to bring in just the largest bones."

The professionals may have been satisfied, but volunteers and news media representatives wanted something more dramatic. "Call me when you find something big," one journalist said. Their desires soon were fulfilled.

On Thursday May 23, a femur, or upper leg bone, was discovered near a group of three markers. That excavation was an extension of a site worked a year earlier that had yielded another leg bone. The archeologists believed all the bones came from the same individual. That supported their theory that only one man had been buried in sites where two markers had been placed.

More interesting finds were ahead. A nearly complete arm was uncovered on Friday May 24 by Fike and Winchell in another east side excavation pit. Other bones ranged from numerous skull fragments to a tail bone and teeth.

The next week on Wednesday May 29, Winchell and Connor, along with volunteers, made what many consider the most dramatic discovery of either archeological project. At Marker 128, an isolated site on Greasy Grass Ridge, on a day when the wind howled and the sun burned brightly, a lower leg bone came into view. Nearby, a shovel struck a ridge of boot leather. Speculation grew that the leg bones would extend inside the boot itself. Even as that proved to be the case, further careful scraping inches away in the dig site revealed a pit with a large collection of jumbled bones.

The site, about 200 yards from the road, just ahead of the south gate, became a favorite target for photographers, amateur and professional. At one point, photographers representing *National Geographic*, *USA Today* and the *Billings Gazette* maneuvered around each other and large numbers of tourists.

Excavation proceeded meticulously, every step faithfully recorded and photographed. In two days of digging, some 150 bones were found. Larger bones included those from the pelvis, ribs, jaw and legs, mixed with fragments of skull and teeth. As Connor said, "We've got pieces from the tip of the toes to the top of his head."

(The human body has about 206 or 207 bones.)

Under her system for designating each excavation, this was "M" site and the remains were later dubbed "Trooper Mike."

What accounts for a nearly complete skeleton being found so long after the battle? "It's probably a secondary burial," Connor explained. More than likely the man had been killed there and haphazardly buried in 1876. The 1877 reburial party overlooked his right leg and boot, but collected the other bones in a hole near the present marker. However, in 1881, troops who moved the dead to Custer Hill monument, for some reason, overlooked "Mike." In 1890, those installing the first marble markers detected enough indication of a burial to place one there, without realizing Mike still rested at the site, so far from his 7th Cavalry comrades.

Equally exciting as the discovery itself were slash marks on the femurs, or upper leg bones. History confirmed! The marks were evidence of mutilation.

In an early 1986 letter, Snow summarized his study of Mike's skeleton: "He was about 19-23 years old. There are at least two gunshot wounds of the chest, in addition to a bullet in the left forearm. He was finished off with massive blunt force blows to the skull. Afterwards, the body was mutilated by hatchet or ax blows to the upper legs. Incidentally, he had a congenital defect of the 5th lumbar vertebra which would cause some exceptional discomfort to a cavalryman. My guess is that he would have been particularly sore from the previous 24 hours of heavy riding."

In addition, the soldier probably stood about 5' 8", which made him above average height. The soldiers averaged 5' 7".

Scott also reported that Mike had probably been whacked with knives or hit with arrows, further confirming the historical record that the Custer dead were mutilated. Does such action mean the Indians were vicious? Scott and Fox say no, especially not for the times they lived in. "The mutilations were a cultural expression," Fox explained. "Severing a limb meant killing the spirit. Sometimes it was used to mark a body, like saying, 'I, a Hunkpapa Sioux, killed this enemy'."

All in all, the archeologists directed excavations at 33 markers in two years at Custer Battlefield. Two other finds are noteworthy. Inside Custer Hill on the last weekend of May 1985, Connor and Jim Thorpen found a soldier's hand and wrist. The thumb was missing and the wrist apparently had been broken.

In 1984, an excavation at Markers 9 and 10 along the South Skirmish Line uncovered significant portions of a soldier's upper body, including two nearly complete arms, breast bones and ribs. A *Life* magazine photo of the bones proved startling, but the archeologists say the 1985 body of Mike is more complete.

Is the Lost Company Found?

One aspect of the two Custer Battlefield archeological projects proved frustrating and disappointing. Neither dig produced any evidence of where the 28 missing Company E men are. However, in 1985, geomorphologist Haynes greatly increased chances of finding them in the future.

During both projects metal detecting crews scoured the ravine floor, walls and lip. Few artifacts were found. In 1983, Fox had marked several mound-like forma-

The ghostly hand of a Custer trooper was found virtually intact, except for a missing thumb, in an excavation pit on Last Stand Hill in 1985.

(Sandy Barnard)

Trooper's Mike's lower leg bones were found still attached to his foot bones inside his boot. The upper part of the boot had been cut away by Indians who wanted the leather.

(Sandy Barnard)

Cut marks on the femurs of Trooper Mike revealed the mutilation that his body sustained at the time of his killing during the battle.

(Sandy Barnard)

tions as places to check. With back-breaking effort in 1984, Fox, assisted by volunteers using two gas-powered augers, drilled three-foot post holes about two feet to six feet apart along the base of the ravine's walls, from the terrace overlooking the river to the head wall area. Nothing showed up. No bones. No artifacts.

Scott at times has considered that the Deep Ravine effort amounted to a wild goose chase. Perhaps the bodies were never there,

This finger bone and ring were found in May 1984 near what has traditionally been called the South Skirmish Line on the main battlefield. **(Dan Martinez)**

or perhaps they had disintegrated in the wet, alkaline soil. Fox believes the men are there, but the 1984 failure puzzled him. For 1985 they invited Haynes to try his expert hand. Off the job, he's an easy-going and congenial fellow who has written a book about the Springfield carbine. He's a certified expert on the subject.

On the job, he's an intense, serious man, who reads dirt walls as easily as the rest of us read a page of a book. He says little while at work. I quickly learned to watch and keep a silent mouth whenever I visited the series of 10 trenches he had the battlefield backhoe dig across the ravine floor, from just above the river terrace to just below the present-day head wall. Those nearest the mouth were awesome, up to 15 feet deep where the wall met the floor surface. Nearer the head wall they averaged only several feet deep because the backhoe could not maneuver on a ravine floor still wet from spring run-off. Those trenches were dug from above the lip of the ravine.

On the first day the machine, with Cliff Arbogast, the battlefield's maintenance foreman at the controls, sank up to its wheels in muck. As Haynes, Fox, Arbogast and volunteer Jim Lafollette struggled to walk it out of the ravine over plywood planks, Haynes quipped: "If we lose the backhoe in the mud, at least we have Irwin Lee's metal detector to find it again."

Haynes thoroughly familiarized himself with the battlefield's terrain. Comparing early era photos with present-day terrain features, he noted how little the landscape has changed since the 1880s. In nearly two weeks at the battlefield, Haynes walked its every yard and many surrounding acres beyond park service jurisdiction, including Medicine Tail Coulee. His goal was simple: to determine the ravine's stratigraphy, or layering and composition of the soil, especially its build up since 1876. By determining where the floor was in 1876, he hoped to pinpoint potential sites for archeological excavation.

Haynes quickly determined that not much erosion has occurred in the ravine, which meant that the Company E troopers, if there, are buried much deeper than

Digging Into Custer's Last Stand

Geomorphologist Vance Haynes (R) and archeologist Richard Fox (C), matching early battlefield photos with today's land features, determined the landscape closely resembles that of 1876. Dick Harmon assisted them.

(Sandy Barnard)

previously believed. However, as his trench work produced no trace of the missing men, everyone assumed Deep Ravine would offer no excitement for a second year.

By the dig's last week everyone's level of excitement was dipping. Media interest was waning, too. After a thousand or so cartridges have been recovered, one more is hardly stirring. No startling finds of bones occurred early that week. Participants began the project's clean-up/shut-down phase.

Yet one more eye-opening discovery remained. On Thursday June 6, Haynes, normally tight-lipped while engaged in field work, flipped back his well-worn slouch hat (a reproduction of an 1889 campaign hat), and said, "I think we may have something here."

He was standing in a 6-foot trench, several yards from the ravine's head wall, facing east toward Battle Ridge. To his right, on top of the south bank, stood the now idle backhoe. On his left was the slump area and some distance behind him was the ravine trail crossing.

"We now know where there's another floor — six to eight feet down," he said. He estimated the ravine's total depth in 1876 would have been about 12 feet. "For a man six feet or under that's a hell of a reach to get out of here. This is the Deep Ravine we've been looking for. A deeper floor that's been buried in a very deep ravine. This matches the (historical) concept."

He smiled. Overhead the sun blazed against a high blue sky.

The front page, lead story in the Friday June 7 *Billings Gazette* overstated the case, but rejuvenated the excitement for everyone connected with the project: "Is 'lost company' found?".

In a September 1985 letter to Jim Court, Haynes reported his findings: "It is quite likely that a vertical headcut at least 14 feet deep existed in Deep Ravine at the time of the battle and that this is the cul de sac mentioned in the historical account."

He doubted that the remains of the men had been washed away. "Had they been flushed out by flashy discharge I would suspect more material to have been

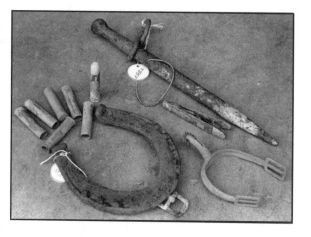

This collection of artifacts was recovered at Reno-Benteen in May 1985. The small wire is actually an Indian bracelet uncovered on Sharpshooter's Ridge where the historical record indicates an Indian marksman fired on the soldiers, claiming several victims.

(Sandy Barnard)

Doug Scott carefully brushes away dirt from the remains of a cavalryman discovered on Greasy Grass Ridge in May 1985. The soldier was dubbed Trooper Mike, because his remains were found in excavation square "M."

(Sandy Barnard)

found on and under the floor of Deep Ravine by both the metal detecting and our trenching. Because so little was found downstream I suspect that much of the remains of Troop E lie buried by several feet of alluvium between the two path crossings, the area Rich and I wanted to test in the first place."

He recommended that "for the proper assessment of the battle history related to Deep Ravine I think that it is essential that the hypotheses regarding Troop E be tested by controlled archeological excavations in Deep Ravine between the two path crossings." He estimated that no more than three 2 x 2 meter test pits would be needed to locate any troop remains.

Digging Into Custer's Last Stand

ASSESSING THE BATTLEFIELD DIGS

Doug Scott conveys the cool image of the professional scientist. Ask how important the Custer project is to him, and he'll respond logically. "It's a project. We gained a lot of information. We made some headway and plowed some new ground for researchers to use. We also used some new techniques so it's a very important project from that standpoint. We've also done something unique at a battlefield ... Custer is an ideal case example to get concepts across to people, and we've developed an entirely new data set."

Great, Doug! How about personally? A pause. The best sheepish grin this side of TV's Richie Cunningham. "It's been neat. It's been a lot of fun for me. It is a high to me."

More seriously, he says the Custer Battlefield archeological digs were important for two reasons. "One is the data and the interpretation that is now going on and which will go on long into the future. Whether some people like or agree with it, it is honest evidence subject to interpretation. The data are there and are a new source of information to be used."

Also, the project has important archeological implications. In the past, historical archeological study has focused on fixed aspects of battlefields — fortifications and gun emplacements, for example — seldom on people's movements and their behavior, out of a belief that humans under combat may not act in patterns that can be readily discerned.

"It's pretty obvious we've turned that idea around. We have learned that the battlefield can yield information and that it is patterned, just like any other human endeavor," he said. "When you fight there is a pattern involved, as random as that pattern may be, but it is still definable. You can still see it in the ground. You can reconstruct it."

Volunteer Tom Switajewski skims the surface with his metal detector along the south path of Reno-Benteen in May 1985.
(Sandy Barnard)

48

A second development for archeology has been the metal detector's significant use as a systematic survey tool. "We've had a positive response from the (archeological) profession. I wouldn't use the metal detector in every circumstance, but it is an important tool."

Tied in with the equipment use was the opportunity to work with people whom he called "avocational archeologists" and "treasure hunters." "Custer just opened it up because of the positive two-way communication that occurred," Scott said.

In discussing their findings, Scott likes to use a crime scene analogy. The criminal investigator first talks to the witnesses for the "oral history" of the event. "Then along comes the forensic investigators who study the crime scene itself and gather the physical evidence of what happened. That's what we're doing. And then you combine the two. You can't have either one by itself and expect it to tell the whole story."

Most important, he said, "We're not trying to re-write history with archeology. We're just adding a new set of physical evidence to a set of oral histories. It gives it a new perspective when you combine the two."

The projects have revealed much about the number and variety of weapons used by the Indians; more about where the Indians took cover and fired at the soldiers; more about how the soldiers were deployed and how they stood and fought; and some about how the troops were dressed and equipped. It's also obvious that the 1881 reburial party did not collect all the parts of the soldiers' bodies.

Regarding Vance Haynes' studies, he said, "Clearly Deep Ravine is not today what it was in 1876. That gives more credibility to the fact the 28 missing men could still be in Deep Ravine or were there. That point still needs study ... (but) we can focus our investigation more precisely."

Clyde Snow's studies of the bones also are enlightening. "The fact that human remains were found near those markers is certainly indicative that the battle took place at that point. Those markers are relatively correct, and that was the purpose of Melissa's project to determine."

Evidence of mutilation detected by Snow verifies what history has long reported. "We can take the height and age data and compare it to Ken Hammer's compilations (*Men With Custer*, The Old Army Press, 1972). That's all verifications of history, and that's nice to have," even if identification of individual soldiers has proved impossible.

"We are more knowledgeable about the kinds of mutilation, and we are learning more about the trooper of the period — height, weight, age and general health. How many traumas or wounds they had."

For example, wear on some teeth was consistent with the pattern of a pipe smoker. Another soldier had been crippled in his leg and likely limped. Another was missing a finger joint, suggesting a prior amputation. Several leg bones had lesions built up over time indicating the men often rode horses, certainly not unexpected for cavalrymen, Scott acknowledges.

"It's detailed data about these individuals. We can build a composite picture of the cavalryman, which is not very far off from the historical record. We can also say that some of these folks had some little physical problems." In the end, a good

Digging Into Custer's Last Stand

Modern 7th Cavalrymen stand as pall bearers during Father Vince Heier's stirring invocation during the reburial service of June 25, 1986. In the background are Indian color guard members of the Lame Deer, Mont., American Legion post.

(Sandy Barnard)

cross-section picture of the American male of the 1870s is being developed.

One disappointment in the research is that skull material was too incomplete in all cases to allow facial reconstruction which could have led to identification of soldiers. Information about their stature isn't enough for identification. Historical records indicate about 60 percent of the soldiers were between 5' 5" and 5' 7" and in their early 20s. Project findings essentially confirmed this.

Snow narrowed some bones to a few possible individuals. "For example, Trooper Mike could be one of 12 people. Knowing he's from Company C narrows it to two or three," Scott said.

The arm found by Rich Fike and Colleen Winchell suggests a man as young as 18. "That person is probably one of two people. Out of 200, to narrow it that close is not bad." However, Scott adds, "To say this is definitively X over Y, we can't."

Are archeological inquires completed at Custer Battlefield?

A quick "no."

Will the project be pursued? "Yes," Scott says, but not before 1987. First, reports and assessments about both digs must be completed.

He says general agreement exists among various parties that "more work remains:" continued probing in Deep Ravine for Company E; additional excavations at battlefield markers, a pet objective for Jim Court; exploring several Reno-Benteen sites to determine whether they were soldier entrenchments. The most important spot historically could be the apparent dump site there.

If additional battlefield archeological work is undertaken, massive use of volunteers, at least on the same scale, probably would be unnecessary. That's no reflection on the people whose talents, energy and time made the first two projects so successful, he stresses. "Volunteers are a useful resource to help archeologists," but future tasks at Custer Battlefield would be more technical and not spread across the countryside as in 1984 and 1985. They would require people, he says, "who can read the dirt."

THE MYSTERIOUS, EXCITING CUSTER BATTLEFIELD

By noon on Saturday June 8, most volunteers had scattered, except for Barbara Ulmanis, Seattle, Wash., and Joy Connor, Melissa's mother from Milwaukee, who were awaiting later air flights. Scott, Connor and graduate student Pat Phillips had left for Lincoln. Under the usual high sun, and rising temperature, the visitor center's parking lot was filling, especially with huge vans and campers of assorted sizes. Park service personnel were going about their duties.

Everyone seemed oblivious to the archeological activities of the previous five weeks. Pinned to the bulletin board just inside the front door were the last *Billings Gazette* story and my last news release, both dated June 7. Occasionally, a tourist scanned them. Inside the book store a display of artifacts from the 1984 dig received an occasional glance.

The excitement was missing. These objects weren't "live." They weren't "in the ground" where they had fallen on June 25, or 26 or 27. As we had seen them during the past five weeks. At that moment I grasped what had made the experience truly memorable for those of us who had been volunteers. Through the rusty dirty metal objects or the human bones, we had glimpsed the Battle of Little Bighorn itself — in a way casual tourists can never. In a way that Custer buffs everywhere can only envy. For us, for five weeks, George Armstrong Custer and his troopers of the 7th Cavalry, and their adversaries, the Plains Indians who defeated them on June 25, 1876, had walked off the pages of the history books and again fought for their lives, on the one hand, and their land, their people and their way of life, on the other, on the ridges and in the coulees above the Little Bighorn River.

The battle was fought anew on the mysterious, exciting plot of ground labeled the Custer Battlefield National Monument.

POSTSCRIPT

Gray clouds softened the sun that earlier in the afternoon had baked the crowd of 2,000 that had gathered in the amphitheater below the Visitors Center on Wednesday afternoon, June 25, 1986. As 4 p.m. neared, their mood, almost festive earlier, turned more somber.

Yet the event that had brought them together was also a cause for celebration, celebration that 110 years after the Plains Indian warriors had overwhelmed Custer's troopers on that very spot, the races could join for a moving burial service for the partial remains of some three dozen troopers found during archeological projects at the Custer Battlefield National Monument. The men included three recovered in 1958 from Reno-Benteen.

Just past 4 p.m., Windy Shoulderblade, who is Cheyenne, and other members of his Lame Deer American Legion Post color guard stepped off smartly down the asphalt path toward the amphitheater, tucked in a little triangle of a valley below Last Stand Hill, the National Cemetery and the battlefield's Visitors Center. Only a steady click of cameras and the sweet chirp of meadowlarks disturbed the silence.

Behind the Indian honor guard, six young soldiers from the Scout Platoon of the modern 7th U.S. Cavalry Regiment struggled with the awkward weight of the flagdraped casket containing the skeletal remains of Trooper Mike and the other 35 of their regimental predecessors. After the posting of colors and the singing of the National Anthem, the Rev. Vincent Heier from St. Louis gave the invocation:

Digging Into Custer's Last Stand

"In one sense, we turn to look back, to look back over a century ago to examine anew the clash of cultures that lead to the people who met here on this field. We honor those who died. In particular those who gave their lives for the country of whom we bury today. Also, we remember those who fought for this land, who fought for what they believed was right," Father Heier said.

He stressed that it is just as important to look to the future. "To look forward to a new age in history. And, what we commemorate should be a sign of the future. That the clash of cultures gave way to a common seeking of peace. That races, religions, creeds and ways of life might stand together and work together in this our land."

Next, Enos Poor Bear, former president of the Oglala Sioux Tribe, spoke about the Indians' perception of the battle anniversary: "We of the Indian nations look upon this battle as one of our finest hours. Let me say in the same breath that if we take from that event only the history that occurred here, we do err."

Only by examining past events can the Indian people fashion for themselves "a better day and a brighter future," he explained.

After speeches by Lorraine Mintzmyer, director of the Rocky Mountain Region of the National Park Service, and Jack McDermott, director of policy for the President's Advisory Council on Historic Preservation, the Scout Platoon, commanded by 1st Lt. John Phalen, carried the casket up the hill to Section B, Grave 402, of the National Cemetery. At the graveside a ceremonial wreath was placed by John White Man Runs, the 92-year-old son of White Man Runs Him, one of Custer's Crow scouts. Father Heier recited the burial prayers of committal.

Off to the side, six members of the Lame Deer legion post raised their rifles. Three volleys echoed across the ridges and coulees. The sounds of Taps, played by John Parle and Lynn Wilke of Peru, N.Y., also rolled across the landscape.

As the modern 7th Cavalrymen, stationed today at Fort Hood, Texas, folded the American flag which had covered the casket, spectators stood in respectful silence, aware of the tragic clash of cultures which years ago had claimed many lives on both sides in this place, now so peaceful.

Reburial Service, June 25, 1986.

(Trevis Mayfield)

Chapter Three

1989 Custer Battlefield Dig

On the first day of the 1989 archeological project, *Billings (Mont.) Gazette* reporter Lorna Thackeray asked archeologist Doug Scott a basic question: "What are you looking for?"

Scott's colleague, Dick Harmon, an expert in frontier period arms, jumped in with a ready answer: "Carbines!"

Meant as a joke, his remark nevertheless summed up a good part of team members' hopes for what they might find in excavating an apparent dump site. Their ultimate haul of hundreds of nails from burned ammunition and ration boxes, metal staples, rings and rivets from saddles and bridles, and buckles made for nice discoveries. But archeologists and volunteers in the 1989 archeological project at the Reno-Benteen Defense Site almost lusted to uncover a Springfield carbine, the primary weapon carried by cavalrymen of the 1870s.

Alas, much to Harmon's disappointment, no carbines were found. Still, Scott and Custer Battlefield Chief Historian Doug McChristian believe the 2,000 artifacts recovered from the dump at Reno-Benteen will aid future interpretation of the Battle of the Little Bighorn. The objects were taken to the National Park Service's Midwest Archeological Center in Lincoln, Neb., for cleaning and lab analysis. That's where some 5,000 other objects were studied after the first two projects of 1984 and 1985.

"A lot is going to come out of the analysis," Scott explained.

During each of his three Custer Battlefield projects, Scott was assisted by a team of archeological experts from Lincoln and several dozen volunteers with expertise in archeology, history, frontier weapons and military gear. The 36 people in the

Digging Into Custer's Last Stand

Irwin Lee, along with his wife, Riva, coordinated the metal detecting efforts during all four of the major archeological projects at the battlefied — 1984, 1985, 1989 and 1994. An expert in the use of metal detectors as an investigative tool, Lee searched the area around Marker 7, just above the old Deep Ravine Trail, on the main battlefield in 1989.

(Sandy Barnard)

The 1989 battlefield project at the Reno-Benteen Defense Site focused on what was believed to have been a 7th Cavalry disposal dump near Water Carrier's Ravine.

(Sandy Barnard)

1989 group were selected from some 250 applicants. The impetus for the battlefield archeological work was a fire in August 1983 that stripped away decades of grasses, brush and undergrowth. Preliminary exploration that month by archeologist Rich Fox led to the more formal projects that Scott and he directed in 1984 and 1985. In 1984, their team scoured the hills and ravines of the main battlefield, relying on metal detectors to locate artifacts used by combatants on either side. In 1985, the quest for battlefield debris shifted to the Reno-Benteen Defense Site.

During both years another activity on the main battlefield involved excavation of 37 of the 252 marble markers that designate where soldiers fell. During these excavations partial skeletal remains of 21 different men were recovered (all in all, the team's forensic anthropologist, Clyde Snow, studied fragmentary remains of 34 men; these included men recovered previously from Reno-Benteen, surface bone discoveries of two men, and bones of eight others that had been held in the battlefield's museum). Soil studies were also conducted around a primary geographical feature called Deep Ravine, where some 28 men, mostly from Custer's Company E, may still be buried.

In 1989, Scott's archeological team focused on excavating what he believed was an equipment disposal site, or dump, used by Reno-Benteen troops after they were relieved by the Terry-Gibbon column on June 27, 1876. History records that the men gathered unserviceable equipment, broke it apart and burned it.

Located during the 1985 metal detecting survey at Reno-Benteen, this site was marked for future exploration. In 1989, the dump was excavated to recover artifacts and to protect it from relic collectors. When the archeological work was completed, a metal grid was installed over the area to make future metal detecting more difficult for looters.

Ironically, Scott said, the archeologists may have been a century or so late. Few large pieces, especially from saddles and weapons, were found. While the presence of so many smaller objects wasn't surprising, he thinks more large pieces should have been uncovered — unless they previously were removed from the dump.

For example, a broken saddle would have been hard for troops in the field to disassemble. If the departing soldiers burned one, "the fire may have charred the saddle but there may have been enough left to pick up," Scott said. "It just appears to me that they (relic collectors) may have been salvaging the best pieces."

The lack of larger items "smacks of a systematic scavenging of the site at some point in the past. Probably not long after the battle," he added. He theorized that early relic collectors, returning Indians or troops from Fort Custer may have picked over the site in the years after the battle.

Scott said that 79 saddle staples were recovered in 1989. Each saddle had four such staples, leading the archeologist to conclude that at least 20 saddles were burned in the dump. The discoveries also aided in answering key research questions Scott had formulated for his 1989 field activity: What kind of gear were the soldiers using during the campaign, and how closely did it follow Army regulations? The dump provided a strong clue about saddles:

"Nothing in the material that we have for 1989 would indicate that saddles were anything but the model 1872. Nothing to indicate that they were 1874," Scott said. The 1872 saddle was a Civil War saddle that was re-covered with leather.

"There is nothing there to indicate that we have the later saddle. I think we can pretty safely say that, at least at the Reno site, these 1872-pattern saddles were being used. That means that the current regulation that had come out in 1874 for that saddle gear was not being used by the 7th Cavalry on that campaign."

The regiment had been outfitted for six months or more from various depots, according to the historical record. Scott said that the lack of the more recent saddle reflects that "the Army was on a tight budget and was just using up the old pattern. So we're seeing the physical evidence, the physical reflection, of government policy."

He points out that arms and ammunition more closely matched Army regulations in effect in 1876. "For campaign purposes, with the horse gear particularly, it suggests that there was a mix and match. With materials that wear out quickly,

Digging Into Custer's Last Stand

The archeological project in 1989 was on a flat below the main defensive perimeter at Reno-Benteen and offered a view of the scene of the opening engagement of Reno's command in the valley below.
(Sandy Barnard)

In 1989 as well as during the other projects at the battlefield, workers had to closely scrutinize the dirt to make certain an artifact wasn't overlooked.
(Sandy Barnard)

John Craig, a veteran of several of the battlefield digs, assisted in recording artifacts accurately.
(Sandy Barnard)

The 1989 Reno-Benteen dig differed from the other projects in that the work concentrated primarily on one locale, but the tasks were just as varied.
(Sandy Barnard)

or probably would be used up more quickly, things were probably more current. But with items that had a longer life span, they would just use them until the unit was ready to replace them. Saddles and horse gear would last a while."

Other small metallic items, especially from ammunition and ration boxes, were found in what seemed to be patterns, often close to the surface. According to historical accounts, such boxes were used to fuel the dump fire. While samples of ammunition boxes are common, ration boxes are not. Drawings and other representations of ration boxes exist, but actual examples are unknown. In studying the artifacts of 1989, Scott has focused on nails.

"We do have several, less than 10, ammunition boxes and/or other boxes represented by those nails," Scott said.

He concludes that some "probably" are ration boxes. "Unfortunately, we are not going to be able to say just exactly how a ration box was constructed. I don't think there is quite enough information to do that, or quite enough evidence from nails in place (in the ground)."

The reason is simple: "The fire at the dump was very effective in destroying all of the wood components. We did find bits of charcoal. Some of it is juniper, which is local wood and which is not unexpected and probably helped fuel the fire. The other woods include poplar and hickory. Poplar and hickory were used in construction of the saddle, and hickory was also used for strapping on ration boxes."

Scott continued: "I can't say anything was definitely a ration box, but there is certainly evidence that some wood of the type used in construction of ration boxes was used to fuel the fire.

"I had hoped to see more nails in patterns, such as in pieces of wood that had not quite burned with the nails still in them, or if the wood had rotted away, there would be nails in pattern. It looks to me as if the fire was very effective. It burned most of the wood and ashed it pretty well."

The early summer of 1876 had been hot in the Little Bighorn region. As a result, Scott believes, "The wood would have been very dry. I suspect it was ready to burn."

In studying materials recovered from the dump, Scott noticed something intriguing about one nail — a piece of lead fastened to its tip. "It could be from a number of different sources, but it's not melted lead. It's not a glob or globule," he said. "It's like a lead scrape, and I'm going to interpret that as a possible bullet that passed through or into one of the boxes and just happened to scrape one of the nails. I think that's the residue of a bullet that hit one of the boxes and that's probably why they were destroying it. We do know that they did use the boxes for barricades.

"If that's the case, there's a little more physical evidence or confirmation of what those folks were saying. Those boxes were damaged and rather than try to haul them back, they took them and threw them in the fire."

Over the years, much speculation has centered on the possibility that the surviving troops may have used multiple dump sites to destroy broken gear. Scott has no doubts about the location found in 1985 and excavated in 1989:

Digging Into Custer's Last Stand

Free-lance writer Neil Silberman (L) was one of many reporters interviewing Doug Scott in 1989.

(Sandy Barnard)

"I think it is definitely a dump site. There is no question in my mind that was what was represented there. Whether or not there are others is open to question. I would think that in all probability there is at least one other."

He said that many people, including long-time Little Bighorn rancher Hank Weibert, have also talked about a dump outside the National Park Service's boundary fence.

"I'm going to take his (Weibert's) word that there is another group of material. So there probably were at least two dump sites, and maybe more than that, out there."

RENEWING THE DEEP RAVINE SEARCH

During the project's third week, Deep Ravine underwent further exploration by Dr. Vance Haynes, a geomorphologist from the University of Arizona who studied the ravine in 1985. Tradition suggests that as many as 28 men, mostly from Company E, were buried where they fell in Deep Ravine in 1876 and that their bodies were never recovered. But despite using a hand auger to bore a series of test holes in the ravine floor in the vicinity of the Deep Ravine Trail Crossing, Haynes discovered no new trooper graves.

However, his work was hindered once again by the high water table. The environment that Haynes faced "was so muddy and so miserable that I'm not certain that we gave it a fair evaluation with that (hand) auger," Scott said.

But lack of information in such situations can be meaningful, he added. "Probably between those two or three sets of holes is where we should concentrate in the future. It was disappointing that we didn't find anything. But in any sort of science, negative information is valuable because it tells you where not to go in the future or what not to do."

What about future projects at Custer Battlefield?

After completing three projects in the 1980s, Scott didn't expect early renewal of archeological work at the battlefield. Still, tasks remain that could benefit from future archeological work. For example, the Deep Ravine questions remain intriguing. Verifying the accuracy of additional marble markers on the battlefield also has promise. However, in the early 1990s, the National Park Service faced larger, more immediate issues. These include addition of a Native American memorial [dedicated in 2003], possible construction of a new visitors center and possible expansion of park boundaries to take in more of the total historical battleground.

"It's really up to park management," Scott said. "What do they want to do? What do they need for interpretation or additional information that can't be gathered through any other source except for archeology?"

McChristian doesn't expect more field work "in the near future," according to the Spring 1990 *Battlefield Dispatch* newsletter of the Custer Battlefield Historical & Museum Association.

"One element visitors appreciate about NPS historic sites is their integrity—they are the real thing," the battlefield's historian wrote. "There is something to be said for leaving at least a portion of the original material in the ground, provided it is not threatened.

In 1989 as well as during the other battlefield projects, archeologist Melissa Connor provided both expert guidance to her crew members and a sure hand with the tools of the trade.

(Sandy Barnard)

"I think that in the case of Custer Battlefield, just knowing that objects are still there—right where they fell in the heat of battle on June 25, 1876—adds immeasurably to its aura."

DISCOVERY OF A CUSTER TROOPER

One aspect of the 1989 field work caught public attention as much as anything had during the two earlier projects. Ironically, 1989's major discovery of a human skull, humerus (arm bone) and clavicle (shoulder bone) during the project's first week was technically outside the dig. The bones were found the morning of May 25 on the west bank of the Little Bighorn River by a dig volunteer, Monte Kloberdanz of Libertyville, Ill. On his own after bad weather forced cancellation of regular field activities for the day, he was exploring the Reno Retreat Crossing. The land is former Crow Reservation property now held by the Custer Battlefield Preservation Committee.

The site's history is well-known to students of the battle. Ordered by Custer to attack the Indian encampment from the south, Major Reno found his advance blunted by heavy pressure from its aroused occupants. He and his men, about

Digging Into Custer's Last Stand

On an off-day for project workers in May 1989, this skull was found along the Little Bighorn River by Monte Kloberdanz. It was later identified as First Sgt. Edward Botzer.

(James Woodcock Billings, Mont., Gazette)

140 strong, first took shelter in woods along a river bend, but soon Reno felt compelled to flee the position. During a poorly executed retreat from the woods, heading east toward the high bluffs across the river, Reno's command sustained a majority of its casualties — 49 killed and 13 wounded.

In 1990, local Montana authorities, assuming the skeletal remains were historical and battle-related, assigned them for initial investigation to Scott's archeological team and McChristian and for eventual study by forensic anthropologist Clyde Snow. Initial field review by the archeologists and by Dr. P. Willey, a forensic specialist at the University of California at Chico and part of the volunteer team that week, suggested that the man had been struck in the face with a heavy blunt object at the time of death.

"There was a severe blunt blow from the right side that came in and sheared off at least three teeth," Willey said at the time. "The crowns were sheared from the roots."

Snow's later study of the skull and other bones in his Norman, Okla., laboratory not only confirmed much of the initial field analysis about the blow the soldier had received, but also added significant detail. Snow suggested that the man was a white male, about 5 feet 8 inches tall — a typical height for a cavalryman of the era. The man was 30 to 40 years old, which would have made him older than most 7th Cavalrymen.

Narrowing the age range still more will be difficult. "We don't have any way to tie that down any tighter right now. There is the possibility of some very detailed bone analysis that we may do a little later on," Scott said.

Snow's study discounted initial speculation about possible arthritis on the man's elbow. While soldiers often developed arthritis from holding reins of their horses for long periods, this trooper did not seem bothered by the condition.

"He was in fairly good health," Scott said. "He did have the trauma where he was whacked in the face, a fracture right above the teeth. Clyde's report didn't notice any more major anomalies. Some wear on his teeth is consistent with the coarse diet of the 19th century."

Most important, Scott added, "There's no evidence to say that it's a modern forensic case. It's too bad that we didn't find some artifacts with it that would be more conclusive, but the circumstantial evidence suggests that he is one of the soldiers."

Scott said that the remains may have been buried in another place and washed down to where Kloberdanz made his discovery. In any case, the bones that were found likely would have been claimed soon by the river.

After Snow's study was complete, the skull was submitted to Betty Pat Gatliff, a forensic expert in sculpture who reconstructed the face using a microscopically correct mold of the actual skull. She built a clay model of the skull which revealed her best opinion about the trooper's facial appearance. The scientifically constructed clay sculpture no longer exists, but her bronze rendition was shown in February 1990 on a TV special, "Custer's Last Trooper," produced by Bill Armstrong for the Arts & Entertainment Network. Armstrong, a veteran Hollywood producer, had a crew at the battlefield during the 1989 dig.

Who was the soldier?

Relying on age as a crucial factor and other historical evidence, the archeological team narrowed the soldier's identity first to a half dozen possibilities, then to two highly probable candidates — Sgt. Edward Botzer of Company G and Pvt. William Moodie (Moody) of Company A. They may have been the only two troopers older than age 30 killed during Reno's retreat from the Little Bighorn Valley. Unfortunately, no known photos of either man were available for comparison to the Gatliff facial reconstruction. (See Chapter 8).

"Without pictures or additional information, we may be out of luck in attempting to confirm the man's identity," Scott said. His cautious approach to identifying the individual stems from experience following earlier discoveries. After previous archeological finds were identified as partial remains of scout Mitch Boyer and Sgt. Miles O'Hara, controversy arose about a possible clash between history and archeology.

"When we identified Boyer and O'Hara, they weren't where they were supposed to be according to history," Scott said.

Still, Battlefield Historian McChristian wrote in the Winter 1990 *Battlefield Dispatch* newsletter that "In an account left by Pvt. Augustus DeVoto, one of the men detailed to retrieve Lt. Benny Hodgson's body, Botzer's corpse was identified among those at the crossing."

According to historical records, Botzer, born in Bremerhaven, Germany, enlisted for the second time on Nov. 26, 1871, at

The day after his discovery of the skull of "Custer's Last Trooper," as the object was dubbed for a television special, Monte Kloberdanz recounted for the news media how he happened on it on the bank just above the river.

(Sandy Barnard)

Digging Into Custer's Last Stand

Perhaps the hardest work during the digs involved the search in Deep Ravine for the remains of missing troopers of Company E. In 1989, Dick Harmon used a multi-section hand auger to bore test holes in the ravine floor.

(Sandy Barnard)

Forensic anthropologist P. Willey (R) has played many valuable roles, both in the field during several of the battlefield projects as well as in the lab studying recovered remains. In 1989, he explained the significance of bone fragments found at Marker 7 near Deep Ravine to volunteer Irwin Lee and archeologist Colleen Winchell.

(Sandy Barnard)

age 26 in Spartanburg, S. C. That would have made him about 31 on the day he died in battle. He was described as having blue eyes, brown hair and a fair complexion. However, his height was listed as 5 feet 6 1/2 inches.

Moodie was also foreign-born. The Edinburgh, Scotland, native enlisted in New York City on Dec. 15, 1874, and was about 35 when killed. Moodie had gray eyes, brown hair and a florid complexion. His height was given as 5 feet 8 inches.

Little more is known about either man, except that each accompanied Reno's command during its unsuccessful attack on the Indian village during the opening phase of the Battle of the Little Bighorn.

Snow also reviewed additional bone materials retrieved from Marker 7 on the main battlefield at the trail crossing of Deep Ravine. The site was partially excavated during the 1984 archeological work, but more bone had since appeared, necessitating further examination. Study of earlier material gathered near this marker revealed a neck vertebra that indicated the man's head had been cut from his body by a heavy, sharp instrument — perhaps a tomahawk or ax.

"All of the pieces that we found there are consistent with the material that we found in 1984. So there's no evidence that there was more than one person buried there," Scott said.

Besides the bone, other artifacts were found in 1989 at the Marker 7 site. "The coin, canteen piece and comb came out of personal possessions and add to the story, but they don't tell us who he was," Scott said.

"We know the guy was an adult between 20 and 35, but so were a lot of those who died that day. Whoever he was, he was decapitated and his skull was crushed. He was a young man, probably in his 20s, but could be as old as his mid-30s. Younger than 35 in all probability. We don't have anything that allows us to narrow it down to any less than 40 or 50 people."

Unfortunately, what would be an important piece of information — the man's height — could not be determined from the bones recovered in either year.

All the human remains discovered in 1989 have been reburied in the battlefield's national cemetery. Remains from the earlier projects were reburied in 1986.

The 1989 project, as the earlier ones, was funded by grants from the Custer Battlefield Historical & Museum Association.

In 1989, Vance Haynes (L) and Dick Harmon experienced a common problem encountered throughout the projects in the search in Deep Ravine for Company E—high water tables and mud.

(Sandy Barnard)

Various artifacts were recovered from the Reno-Benteen disposal dump in 1989. Clockwise, by group, from upper left: tin can; camp boiler lid; saddle nail; cinch ring and box nails; saddle tiedown ring; and saddle buckles.

(Sandy Barnard)

This human molar was recovered from the area around Marker 7 above Deep Ravine in May 1989.

(Sandy Barnard)

Chapter Four

REBUILDING THE CUSTER HOUSE

FORT ABRAHAM LINCOLN

On Saturday June 17, 1989, George and Libbie Custer returned to Fort Abraham Lincoln in North Dakota to again take up residence in the commanding officer's quarters. On the first two historical occasions when they moved in, probably only a few friends were on hand. This time a crowd of several hundred watched as actors portraying the couple cut the ribbon across the front door. Many people lined up for a tour through the tall rooms of the Custers' new quarters.

The event also marked the start of a highly successful year for the sponsoring Fort Abraham Lincoln Foundation. From June 17 through Sept. 20, more than 42,000 people, from every state and 17 foreign countries, toured the Custer House.

"It was phenomenal," said Pat Ness, the foundation's executive director at the time. "In fact, it was beyond our wildest dreams."

It's the third time a house assigned to the Custers has been built on the site west of the Parade Ground of the old military fort, just a stone's throw from today's slower moving, yet still meandering Missouri River. The first was built in 1873 as the centerpiece of seven buildings that formed Officers Row on the fort's western perimeter. Three duplexes sat on both sides of the Custer House.

That original house was destroyed by fire in February 1874. A second, built later in 1874, lasted less than 20 years. It gains its importance as the only house that George and Libbie shared that reflected both their tastes and frontier lifestyle. Libbie Custer wrote about the place: "Of all the happy days, the happiest had now come to us at Fort Lincoln." In this house, they enjoyed a genteel lifestyle despite the harsh realities of the frontier.

This familiar photo shows the Custers entertaining in their house in July 1875. Custer stands behind the woman at the piano; Libbie is seated in the parlor center.
(State Historical Society of North Dakota)

But her happiest moments would be forever entwined with her saddest, for it was from this house and Fort Lincoln, on May 17, 1876, that George Custer led his 7th Cavalry on its tragic march to the Little Bighorn in Montana Territory. It also was in this house, on July 6, 1876, that Libbie Custer received the sad news that her Boy General and 267 of his men had died fighting the Sioux and Cheyenne.

Fort Lincoln was abandoned by the government in the 1890s, and by 1900 no structures remained at the site. The third Custer house was the culmination of the dreams of people in the state's historical society and the preservation committee. The restored Custer home isn't about battles that Custer fought and won or the controversy surrounding his tragic defeat. Instead, it shows off the lifestyle of the legendary cavalry officer and his beloved Libbie.

INSIDE CUSTER HOUSE

You approach the home from the east, walk up the broad front steps and cross a porch that extends along the front and down the north side. Once inside the front door in a long hall, you are transported back to the 19th century. The house, outfitted as authentically as possible, is based on photos, archeological research and writings of Libbie Custer and others. Few objects in the house are Custer originals, since many of those are in the hands of private collectors and would be prohibitively expensive to obtain.

A few steps to the left of the hallway, on the south side of the home, is the parlor with bay window that wasn't called for by original Army designs, but was much desired by the Custers. Clay pots similar to originals can be seen.

Rebuilding the Custer House, Fort Abraham Lincoln

In *Boots and Saddles*, Libbie commented that "It was a palace compared with what we had been accustomed in other stations, and I know we were too contented to give much thought to what the house lacked."

Above the first fireplace hangs a picture of George, Libbie and the general's brother, Tom. A table holds a stereopticon with vintage photos of Washington, D.C. A $4,000 cherrywood grand piano, whose design dates from 1870, has a music stand stocked with pieces that would help the residents pass the long hours on the frontier. The piano, a replica of the one Libbie played, dominates the parlor where brocaded portieres believed to be from the original Custer Home outline the tall windows.

"The portieres over the curtains in the parlor were Libbie Custer's," Ness said. "It's amazing what we've had donated from that period of time, what came out of attics and basements."

Two sisters from Washington State donated the portieres that hang in the parlor and at the top of the steps. Their grandfather reportedly served at the fort in 1873 and married a cook there. When the couple left, they supposedly took the curtains that had been hanging in the Custer house.

Down the long parlor, past the piano and a harp, is the dining room with a crisp cloth and silver condiment set. Another original object the foundation has of Libbie Custer's is described by Ness as "a great big ironstone turkey platter."

Across the central hallway from the parlor are Custer's library, the master bedroom and a dressing room. In a corner of the library stands a replica of Custer's desk, made by Duncan Warren of Mandan, N. D., based on a photo and sketchy dimensions. Libbie's chair is beside it. A buffalo head hangs over the fireplace. Other walls hold portraits of figures important in Custer's life — Generals George McClellan and Philip Sheridan and actor and friend Lawrence Barrett.

Against another wall rests a couch covered with a blanket that recalls another Libbie Custer comment: "On a wide lounge at one side of the room my husband used to throw himself down on the cover of a Mexican blanket, often with a dog for his pillow."

Furniture in the master bedroom came from Fort Lincoln, but whether it was used by the Custers is unknown.

"The bedroom set in the Custer bedroom we know was at the fort at the time the Custers were there, but we cannot prove conclusively it was their's," Ness said.

Perhaps the most important item in the house that can be traced to the Custers is the general's military field desk.

A visitor to the restored home climbs the stairs to the second floor while holding a railing (balustrade) made of butternut, a difficult wood that required 80 hours of labor to bring out its richness. Custer reportedly insisted on such detail because he had admired similar stairways in grand mansions he visited in the South during the Civil War.

On the north side is a long room aptly described again by Libbie herself: "Upstairs there was a long room for the billiard table, and we had sleeping rooms and servants' rooms besides."

The billiard table is ready for play, although no cues of the period have been found.

In the 1870s, the Commanding Officer's Quarters dominated Officers Row west of

Rebuilding a home on the site has long been a cherished goal of people in the Bismarck area, but the effort, going back to the 1950s, endured many on-again, off-again moments.

"Finally in 1980, a group of people decided now is the time," Ness explained.

A non-profit Fort Lincoln Foundation was formed with the goal of reconstructing five buildings at the fort, including the Custer House that would go on the exact site of the original commanding officer's quarters. Ness, executive director since 1987, said that many doubted the project's potential for success, but by June 17, 1989, the rebuilt house had become a reality. "The Custer House itself stands from private donors, some corporate donors and a whole lot of gutsy work by a lot of people," Ness said.

She laughed, then added, "It's amazing. Custer House was built almost on a day to day basis, as the money was raised. It's really a testimony to a real effort by a lot of people who knew how important it was to this area. Now we have some

the parade ground at Fort Abraham Lincoln.

(State Historical Society of North Dakota)

national interest, some congressional interest. The North Dakota Parks and Recreation Department has been wonderful."

The state parks department oversees Fort Lincoln State Park, but the Fort Lincoln Foundation leases Cavalry Square, a rectangular area directly in front of the house that includes the original parade ground, from the department. "The foundation is responsible for the reconstruction and fund-raising efforts," Ness explained.

Total development for Cavalry Square could cost as much as $6 million, an effort bolstered by $2 million appropriated by the U. S. Congress. The Custer House itself cost nearly $400,000. As in historical times, the house will be the centerpiece, but the foundation plans to reconstruct four other buildings — the commissary storehouse, central barracks, guardhouse and granary.

"We hope to have all five buildings finished by 1994, with fund raising efforts to continue so that we might reconstruct some of the officers homes on either side of the Custer House," Ness said.

Digging Into Custer's Last Stand

In 1989, archeologist Fox, who previously had studied the site of the house, had another team in the field studying the commissary site. "In this kind of situation, archeology is of prime importance," Ness says. "It always raises questions but it answers them, too." The Custer House reconstruction benefitted significantly from Fox's earlier work. "We found the original cellar," she noted. Also, cornerstones erected by the Civilian Conservation Corps in the 1930s were confirmed as inaccurate.

"Another thing is that they were able to tell us so much because the first house burned, and then the other house, the one we have recreated, was constructed and they were able to tell us the period of time and that kind of thing."

Fox planned another field season in 1990 to explore the barracks site on the east side of Cavalry Square and to dig test pits for pilings for the commissary storehouse. Ness expected construction to start on the storehouse by mid-summer 1990; the foundation plans to use the 200 x 24-foot building as a visitors center in 1991. Depending on Fox's findings and the weather, construction on the barracks would begin in fall 1990.

That would leave just the guardhouse and granary to be completed in the future. However, given the magic and legend of the Custer name, the house will remain the focal point in the years to come.

(Note: See Chapter Five for more information about the buildings at Fort Lincoln today.)

History of the Original Custer House

The Custer House is tied irrevocably to the history of its surrounding area. In the years after the Civil War, the nation, realizing the value of rail travel, made building railroads a priority. Businessmen launched numerous efforts to stretch iron rails across the country through largely unexplored or uninhabited territory. In the upper tier of northern states, the Northern Pacific Railroad received a charter to construct a line from Duluth, Minn., across Dakota and Montana territories to Puget Sound in Washington State. By early June 1873, the railhead had reached Bismarck, Dakota Territory, where construction stalled for the rest of the decade as a result of the financial panic of that year.

Even with construction halted, exploration of a route continued. By fall 1873, railroad surveyors had reached the confluence of the Yellowstone and Big Horn rivers. Unfortunately for the NPRR, surrounding lands belonged to the Indians, some of whom were considered "hostile" to the white man's use of their lands. With conflict inevitable, the Army sought to protect the rail crews. To provide logistical support, the War Department strengthened its holdings in the Upper Missouri River region.

In 1872, Fort McKeen was established as an infantry garrison. It was situated on the west bank of the Missouri River, only a few miles downstream from Bismarck. But infantry troops were no match for the highly mobile Sioux, "the Cavalry of the Plains." Fort McKeen, soon renamed Fort Abraham Lincoln, was enlarged to house the 7th U. S. Cavalry, commanded by Lt. Col. George Armstrong Custer.

The original commanding officer's quarters at Fort Abraham Lincoln wasn't used for long by the Custers, as it burned in February 1874. The drawing depicts the house's interior.
(State Historical Society of North Dakota)

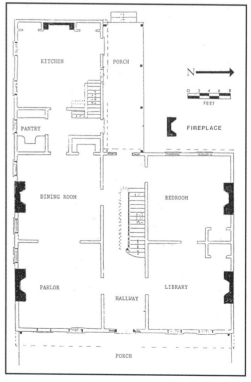

After the fire, the Custers' house was rebuilt and customized by them. This version was identified by archeologist Richard Fox as House 2a.

(State Historical Society of North Dakota)

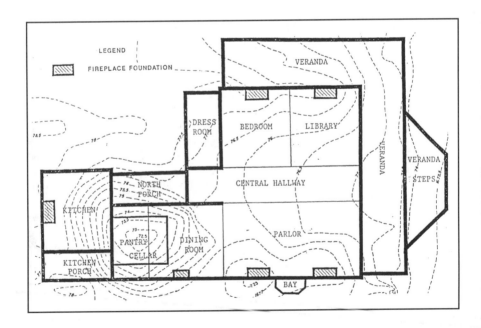

Rebuilding the Custer House, Fort Abraham Lincoln

Construction began in spring 1873 and many buildings, including the commanding officer's house, were ready for occupancy by winter.

Custer and much of his unit had spent the summer with Gen. David S. Stanley's command providing escort duty for NPRR surveyors in Montana. The house wasn't quite ready when the troops returned in September, but in November Custer and his wife moved in. Their occupancy of this first residence proved short, as it was destroyed by fire on Feb. 6, 1874. While awaiting construction of their new house, the Custers lived with his brother Tom in one of the duplexes along Officers Row.

According to a study of the Custer House history and the site by archeologist Fox, the original building contained four 16-foot by 16-foot rooms in the main partition. After the fire, blueprints approved by the secretary of war called for a $4,000 house to be built with troop labor. "The blueprints were not followed precisely in building the replacement house," Fox said. But he could find no official reason for any changes, and concluded that "It does seem ... that the Custers were involved in some way with the changes. Libbie wrote that the General was taken up with the task of planning the interior. And Libbie requested and received a bay window that opened from the parlor. Other additions included an enlarged porch or veranda and a kitchen addition."

Fox also determined that construction probably wasn't completed until summer 1874, which would have meant that Custer himself was away. He had left with his troops from Fort Lincoln on July 1 on his Black Hills Expedition, famous for its discovery of gold, and did not return until Aug. 30.

"Nevertheless," Fox said, "judging from Libbie's memoirs she and her husband left their personal stamp on the final configuration" of this second house. The planning probably took place before he left for the Black Hills.

Sometime following the Custers' occupancy of the house, a ballroom addition was built on the south side and required the removal of Libbie's bay window. That change and others increased the square footage from the 3,500 of the Custer period to nearly 5,000.

The house actually did not have a long history. Libbie moved out soon after her husband's death, and a new commander took over later that summer. The fort became regional army headquarters for the Department of the Dakota, and by 1878, the department's ordnance depot was housed there to support frontier operations. But the Army's evolving western mission spelled changes for the fort's own role. In 1882, regional headquarters was moved to Fort Meade in present-day South Dakota. In 1891, Fort Lincoln was decommissioned, less than 20 years after it was built.

"Custer House, once an imposing edifice by Dakota prairie standards, was dismantled by local folk as they salvaged construction materials," Fox said. "By the turn of the century Custer House, and other post buildings, no longer existed. The fort site languished in obscurity until the 1930s when the Civilian Conservation Corps brought their make-work projects to old Fort Abraham Lincoln."

The CCC marked the sites of former buildings, including the Custer House, and made other improvements in what had become a state park. In 1966, archeologist Clyde Dollar extensively excavated the site, but the project was scuttled before completion and he never issued a final report.

Fox labeled this building as House 2b, enlarged as it was after the Custers' occupancy to include the south ballroom addition.

(State Historical Society of North Dakota)

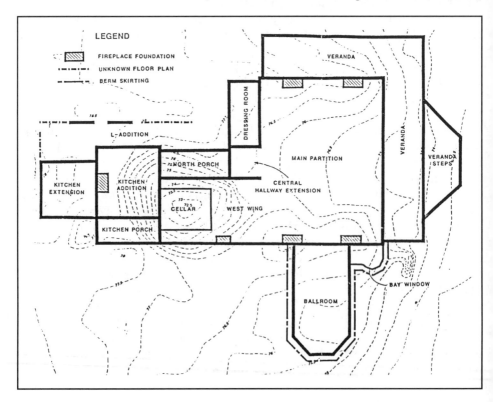

Still, both the desire for unraveling any mystery about the house and the goal of rebuilding it continued. The North Dakota Parks and Recreation Department's master plan envisioned a multi-year program to upgrade facilities and improve historical interpretation at the site. Important to the latter task was reconstruction of several fort buildings, including the Custer House. The Fort Lincoln Foundation, a private, non-profit or-

As the Army's mission changed on the frontier by the 1890s, Fort Lincoln became less important and was closed in 1891. By the end of the 1890s, materials used in the house had been recycled by local residents.
(State Historical Society of North Dakota)

ganization, was established to assist the parks department with the task.

Before any reconstruction could begin, the area had to be excavated to recover historical artifacts and gain insight into the house's appearance. In his field study, Fox determined that, in effect, three houses had occupied the site:

- 1873's original that burned;
- 1874's reconstructed house that the Custers lived in;
- Post-Custer era's expanded house.

Fox concluded that the Custer House was built in three evolutionary phases. The original house, completed in late 1873, burned a few months later in February 1874. What Fox called House 2a is the one most identified with the Custers, because, as it was being built during spring and summer of 1874, several features important to George and Libbie Custer were incorporated into the structure. House 2b involved the same building, as remodeled by other occupants and the Army in the years following Mrs. Custer's departure.

Fox's archeological exploration determined that House 1 matched closely the Army's original plans for a "main building 42 by 33.5, 4 rooms 16 by 16, rear building (west wing) 17 by 25." However, the veranda was only 8-feet deep in the original house and extended only across the front or east side of the house, not its north side. The veranda steps were much smaller, and toward the rear, a porch on the north was longer than specified.

The four interior rooms on the first floor measured 16 feet square, with two on each side of an 8-foot central hallway. The northwest room likely was the Custers' bedroom, the northeast room served as the library, the southeast room was the parlor, while the southwest room was the dining room. Each room apparently relied on its own fireplace for heat.

Modern photos show the interior of the restored Custer House, including the kitchen (top), the master bedroom (middle) and the parlor. Although dating from the historical period, the bed didn't belong to the Custers.
(Sandy Barnard)

To the rear, or in the west side wing, an 8-foot by 16-foot pantry separated the dining room from the 16-foot square pantry. Abutting the west wall of this west wing was a kitchen fireplace, although any evidence of its existence had been lost previously. From this configuration Fox developed a basis for analyzing the evidence and determining the layout and appearance of the longer term Custer home.

He emphatically stated that "It is apparent from the archeological evidence that Custer House 2a was built precisely atop the remains of House 1, at least that portion that coincided with House 1."

The dining room of the modern Custer House
(Sandy Barnard)

He added that the configuration for the original house with its main partition and west wings was duplicated in the rebuilt structure.

"It is the outline of these components that coincide in the ground. And it is the additions to the House 2a main partition and west wing that distinguish it from House 1."

The veranda saw one of the primary changes. Only 8-feet deep in the original, it became 10-feet deep in the successor and extended not only across the east front but also around the corner and down the north side. Fox notes that Mrs. Custer had commented that the couple had enjoyed such a "piazza" while living in the south after the war.

Libbie also gained her bay window. She wrote that the "window broke the long line of the parlor (and) varied the severe outline of the usual type of army quarters." However, Fox said, the bay window's existence could not be proved archeologically because it was built well above ground.

Custer's study in the restored house
(Sandy Barnard)

Digging Into Custer's Last Stand

Custer (Steve Alexander) and Libbie (Amber Gross) at their piano in June 1996. **(Sandy Barnard)**

Fox, citing Libbie Custer's writings as his source, concludes that "the major metamorphosis of Custer House 2a emerged from the new interior room plan that was apparently devised by General Custer." He also cites Mrs. Custer as a primary source for determining the layout of the rooms:

"On one side of the hall were the general's library, our room, and dressing room. The parlor was opposite, and was thirty-two feet in length. It opened with sliding doors into the dining room, and still beyond was the kitchen."

Fox believes the two north-side rooms the bedroom and library — remained the same, but the house had an 8-foot by 16-foot dressing room added on the west. This room opened into the Custers' bedroom.

On the south side of the house, the parlor was doubled in size — from 16 x 16 to 16 x 32 — to include the area of the dining room in the first house. The dining room essentially supplanted the area of the pantry in the west wing, probably taking up the first 16 feet of the west wing. As evidence, Fox points to a fireplace foundation within the dining room that did not exist in House 1.

The pantry probably was placed within the remaining space of the west wing and measured 8 by 16 feet. With no room in the structure for the kitchen, one had to be added on to the rear of the west wing. He expects a new fireplace was needed in that new room.

In summary, Fox stated: "Custer House 2a, therefore, emerged as a variation on the House 1 theme except the ground floor interior was so drastically rearranged that the kitchen addition was necessary. The enlarged veranda, its steps, the parlor bay window and the dressing room emerged in House 2a. So we can feel reasonably certain that these components existed on May 17, 1876. In fact, they seem to be the result of the personal touch of George and Libbie Custer, active as they were in designing their new home."

In addition, he said, "We can feel reasonably sure as well that the north porch, the porch on the north side of the west wing, was included in the new House 2a."

Rebuilding the Custer House, Fort Abraham Lincoln

On the south side, a porch off the kitchen, evident in historical photos, likely was constructed at the time, giving the Custer house three porches in all — the veranda on the east and north sides, a north porch tucked between the dining room and dressing room, and the kitchen porch.

For the times and place, the house that George and Libbie Custer built and lived in was rather elegant, and certainly served them well as the post's commanding officer and first lady.

Fox believes that three other components of House 2b probably came after the Custers — a kitchen extension, the ballroom off the parlor and the L-addition on the north side. But proving that from the archeological evidence was difficult. About the ballroom, he is certain that if it had been built during Libbie's occupancy, she surely would have mentioned it in her book, especially since it would have required the removal of her beloved bay window in the parlor.

From paint fragments discovered by his team, Fox developed conclusions about the colors of the interior rooms. The ballroom, for example, likely was painted an off-white. The dining room may have been a two-tone blue/gray and rose. Beige and rose specimens were found in the area of the add-on dressing room and the Custers' bedroom. Out back in the kitchen addition area, he found beige and off-white paint fragments. However, he cautions that the plaster fragments could also have come from upper story rooms.

White pine shingles likely were affixed to the roof by 3d and 4d nails. Pine appears to have been the predominant lumber type used in constructing the house.

Before any of the buildings were rebuilt on their original sites at Fort Abraham Lincoln, archeological crews carefully examined the areas to determine their historical significance.
(Sandy Barnard)

Digging Into Custer's Last Stand

Shiplap siding of hard maple likely was used on the sides of the house. Most of the brick probably came from the Bismarck area, although some with St. Louis markings may have been imported.

One of the more intriguing aspects of the archeological work involved the cellar. He has no doubt that it was constructed with House 1 and likely excavated for use with House 2a and 2b. From the Custers, it is known that a wildcat captured by the general during his 1873 Yellowstone expedition dwelled for a period in the cellar. While some evidence of burned materials was found in the cellar and might suggest that it was used as a post-fire dump, Fox doubts such a theory.

At Fort Lincoln State Park archeologist Richard Fox (L) provided an experienced guiding hand, first in 1986 excavating the Custer House site (rebuilt, in background), and again in 1989 at the site of the Fort Lincoln Commissary, since rebuilt.

(Sandy Barnard)

Chapter Five

FORT ABRAHAM LINCOLN TODAY

George Custer, in the person of Steve Alexander, often revisits his restored home at Fort Abraham Lincoln State Park.

(Sandy Barnard)

Views of the restored Custer House, Fort Abraham Lincoln.

(Sandy Barnard)

Fourteen years have passed since the Custer House was rebuilt on Cavalry Square at Fort Abraham Lincoln. Since then, the house has become a popular tourist attraction, drawing 40,000 or more people annually to the site. Helping to attract them are additional historic buildings reconstructed on the square since 1989. These are the Commissary Storehouse, which serves several purposes, including as a meeting place and as a store front for the Fort Lincoln Foundation; the Granary; and a Cavalry Barracks building. One other building originally planned was the guardhouse, but funds ran out before it could be constructed, explains Tracy Potter, who succeeded Pat Ness as the organization's executive director in 1993. "Archeology just cost more than we expected," he says.

Lt. Col. and Mrs. George Armstrong Custer, June 1996.
(Sandy Barnard)

The guardhouse may yet be built, as the foundation contemplates the site's future. "We are in the planning stages of Phase II of the rebuilding, and the guardhouse stays on the plate as something that we may do," he says. "We've discussed other alternatives to other buildings that we could use there."

Other possibilities include the post theater, stables, hospital and quarters of the Arikara scouts. No matter what buildings come along, they also will date from the 1875 period. "Probably a majority of the people want us to remain in the 1875 genre," Potter says. "So whatever building it is, it won't be something that was built in 1878. It will have existed at the fort on the location that we have rebuilt in 1875."

One of the early decisions made as the Custer House itself was being built concerned how to portray it to the public. That led to rooting the living history program in 1875. "So all the tours in the Custer House since 1989 have been by tour guides in character in uniform as either housekeepers or laundresses or soldiers of the 7th Cavalry."

The guides usually account for the Custers' absence from the fort. "The Custers unfortunately are not home right now," the guides will tell visitors. "They'll be back soon. Are you a friend of the general's?"

Occasionally, a reenactor, such as Steve Alexander, nationally known for his portrayal of George A. Custer, will be present in historical garb to greet visitors.

Across the parade ground looking north at today's Fort Lincoln stands the restored Granary. On the southern edge of the parade ground is the Commissary, which functions as the visitors center and meeting room for the state park today.

(Sandy Barnard)

All in all, Potter suggests, "We really try to bring people back to 1875."

Changes have occurred in the living history program over the years. Initially, guides focused on the Custers and their house, and emphasized the life of the fort's commanding officer in the Victorian era. But since completion of the other buildings, notably the cavalry barracks in 1993, visitors gain insight into the life of enlisted men in the period. They may even be greeted by grumbling troopers of the 7th Cavalry.

The north wing of the barracks building is where troopers of the living history program greet tourists. The south wing is set up as an open museum, where biographies of enlisted men of the 7th Cavalry's Company M attached to the bunks add historical flavor. The historical Company M actually was assigned to Fort Rice down the Missouri River from Fort Lincoln in 1875, but the Fort Lincoln Foundation chose it for a particular reason. "We wanted a company that was in the Little Bighorn fight, but the majority of whose men survived. That would give us a variety, rather than having dead, dead, dead on every bunk," Potter explains.

Just as the buildings are reconstructions of the originals, much of their contents are replicas. "I don't seek museum pieces so much," Potter explains. "I am interested in replica items, particularly because of our openness. If someone steals a replica, I'm not so concerned. We kind of like using it [the fort] as a teaching institution."

The facility is open year-round, but actual hours vary by season.

Beyond today's granary still rise the bluffs that Custer and the 7th U.S. Cavalry climbed on May 17, heading on the campaign that would end at the Little Bighorn less than six weeks later.

(Sandy Barnard)

The restored Enlisted Men's Barracks at today's Fort Abraham Lincoln. Period dress and other artifacts are shown in the barracks and its mess area, as they might have looked in 1876.

(Sandy Barnard)

By late summer 2003, a reconstructed stables (top, middle) had been finished at Fort Lincoln. As seen in the bottom photo, it sits on the site of an original stables by the Missouri River. A cluster of modern park maintenance buildings also can seen at the river's edge. Across the road is the barracks, while on the right is the commissary. The Custer House roof and chimneys are visible by the finger bluff on the right, while the granary's roof may be seen beyond the brush in the photo's center.

(Sandy Barnard)

Digging Into Custer's Last Stand

In May of 1876, Lt. Col. George Armstrong Custer led his 7th U.S. Cavalry Regiment up through the ravine in the center of the top photo. They left Fort Abraham Lincoln on a campaign that would result in a disastrous attack six weeks later on a huge Indian village encamped in the valley of the Little Bighorn River. Custer and many of his men would never see old Fort Lincoln again.

(Sandy Barnard)

Chapter Six

CUSTER'S BIRTHPLACE

NEW RUMLEY, OHIO

Birthplace of George Armstrong Custer, Dec. 5, 1839
(Little Bighorn Battlefield National Monument)

Emmanuel Custer
**(Little Bighorn
Battlefield National
Monument)**

Maria Custer
**(Little Bighorn
Battlefield National
Monument)**

In New Rumley, Ohio, on Dec. 5, 1839, George Armstrong Custer was born, the third child of Emmanuel and Maria Custer. The house in which his birth cries echoed was already 22 years old. It had been built as a two-story log structure with a kitchen attached to the back by James G. Ward in 1817.

That August, according to the book, *Custer's Ohio Boyhood*, by Charles B. Wallace, Ward began operating part of his building as a tavern. In 1823, Ward's daughter, Maria, married Israel R. Kirkpatrick, a New Rumley merchant. In 1830, after several members of her family, including her parents, had died, Maria and her husband moved into her father's old tavern house.

Also members of New Rumley's tight-knit community were blacksmith Emmanuel Custer and his wife Matilda. The year 1835 was crucial for both Emmanuel Custer and Maria Kirkpatrick, as both lost their spouses. A year later, they married and took up residence in her big

Custer statue, Custer Memorial Park, New Rumley, Ohio. The statue was dedicated June 22, 1932.
(Sandy Barnard)

house, which her first husband had improved by the addition of a frame storeroom on the southeast side and clapboard siding. George, their third baby, was born in the back bedroom on the ground floor and was their first child to survive.

In the next 12 years, the couple would see three more sons and a daughter born: Nevin in 1842, Tom in 1845, Boston in 1848, and Margaret (Maggie) in 1851. In 1876, Tom and Boston would die near their older brother George on the ridge above the Little Bighorn, leaving Nevin as the sole surviving Custer son.

Wallace writes in his book, "About the time Boston was born, Emmanuel Custer was seriously considering a whole new vocation and a move from the big grey house where he and Maria had lived for more than a dozen years."

In April 1849, Emmanuel sold the house and moved the family to an 80-acre farm he had bought in North Township about three miles northwest of New Rumley. Although the Custers were gone, the house itself apparently stood on the lot until 1894.

This third Custer site has seen less archeological field activity than the Montana battlefield and Fort Lincoln, but the people behind the efforts have been just as enthusiastic about their task. The place where George Custer was born has long

Digging Into Custer's Last Stand

Archeologist Don Bier believes the Custer house sat closer to the road, not on the sunken foundation to his rear.

(Sandy Barnard)

been a state park — Custer Memorial Park — but its upkeep has always been a problem. The one-acre park has included a larger-than-life statue of Custer, the cellar foundation of a house believed to have been the Custer family's, and an outdoor historical display. So in April 1986 the Custer Memorial Association was established to promote the birthplace site as a viable tourist attraction. According to the CMA, the park "had literally been put in the attic of Ohio's historical sites."

Thanks to the CMA and the Ohio Historical Society, today the park is regaining a measure of prominence. A 1987 feasibility study recommended that a visitors center and museum be built. The Ohio State Legislature in 1988 appropriated $200,000 for capital improvements. The CMA also helped raise funds to assist in completing the $600,000 project.

As part of the improvements project, Don Bier, an archeologist from the Ohio Historical Society, conducted studies at the park. Bier leans strongly toward the idea that the existing cellar foundation in the park, set some distance from the roadway, was not necessarily that of the Custer house built in 1817. During field work in summer 1989, he discovered a line of stone blocks close by state Highway 646 that runs in front of the park. He thinks that feature marks either a fence line for the Custer house or an actual foundation line for the house. He's optimistic that photo analysis of the site may confirm his theory that the traditional cellar foundation did not belong to the Custer house of the 1840s.

While he can't guarantee that he has properly placed the Custer house on the lot, he thinks an "intact cultural deposit" of ceramic materials and buttons found in the vicinity of the stone blocks provides strong support for his theory.

"It's the right time period for the Custer occupation" of the structure, he says.

On the other hand, in the cellar foundation area, the only debris he found was more recent and not historical. Also, his investigation of other random areas in the park revealed only items of the late 19th or early 20th centuries. Finally, conversations between Bier and older residents of the New Rumley area about their recollections of the Custer site provide more support for his theory that the house may have sat closer to the front of the lot by the roadway, not on the cellar foundation.

"All of this stuff just falls together," he said.

Undoubtedly, in the 1840s, a young George Custer roamed the hills that lay behind the property owned by his father, Emmanuel.

(Sandy Barnard)

After the archeological project was completed in 1989, the Custer Memorial Park was completely renovated. A brick-edged patio outlines the presumed site of the Custer house and historical panels tell of his life and career.

(Sandy Barnard)

Digging Into Custer's Last Stand

Unfortunately, for reasons of time and money, no further archeological work has been conducted to prove his theory. In the earlier 1990s, additional capital improvements scheduled for the park were completed. These included filling in the foundation area and building a multi-tier patio over it. The patio cover outlines the likely layout of the house. Historical exhibits that were erected describe highlights of Custer's life and career.

Even though the construction overlapped what Bier thought might have been the house's actual site, he was optimistic during his field work in 1989 that promising areas for future archeological exploration wouldn't be entirely compromised.

As for other areas in the park, he was less optimistic. "I came to the realization that even though I would like to do more digging, as much as the area (of the park) has been modified, I don't know what we would find."

His conclusion was actually a familiar one where George Armstrong Custer is concerned: Digging into the mysteries about the life and legend of Custer leads to endless inquiries but far fewer provable conclusions.

During his 1989 work at the Custer Birthplace site in New Rumley, Ohio, archeologist Don Bier wondered whether the actual structure sat closer to the hamlet's main road.

(Sandy Barnard)

Chapter Seven

THE DIG OF 1994

LITTLE BIGHORN BATTLEFIELD

In 1994, the first week of May once again found archeologist Doug Scott surrounded by eager volunteers, armed with their metal detectors and their enthusiasm for searching the rugged countryside in and around Little Bighorn Battlefield National Monument.[1] The battlefield dig of 1994, conducted between May 2 and 13, operated much the same way as previous searches. Metal detector professionals with their equipment listened for tell-tale pings that signaled a metal object lay beneath the surface of the battlefield. Pin flags were inserted on the site of a "hit" and another group, or recovery team, meticulously uncovered the object, whether an artifact possibly tied to the Custer-Indian fight of 1876 or a soft drink can more recently discarded. If Scott or another project expert made a field determination that the object had likely ties to the battle, electronic gear recorded its exact placement on the ground.

His 1994 equipment may have been more sophisticated than what Scott used in 1984's opening round of archeological projects at Little Bighorn but the 28 volunteers featured many familiar faces from previous battlefield crews. For example, the metal detector crew chiefs were again Irwin and Riva Lee. Scott was assisted by Dr. Peter Bleed, Stan Parks, Karin Roberts and Dr. Effie Anathnassopoulos of the University

---

[1]Material for this chapter was derived from interviews with Doug Scott as well as from his report on the 1994 dig: Scott and Peter Bleed, *A Good Walk Around the Boundary, Archeological Inventory of the Dyck and Other Properties Adjacent to Little Bighorn Battlefield National Monument,* (Lincoln, Neb.: Nebraska Association of Professional Archeologists and the Nebraska State Historical Society, 1997).

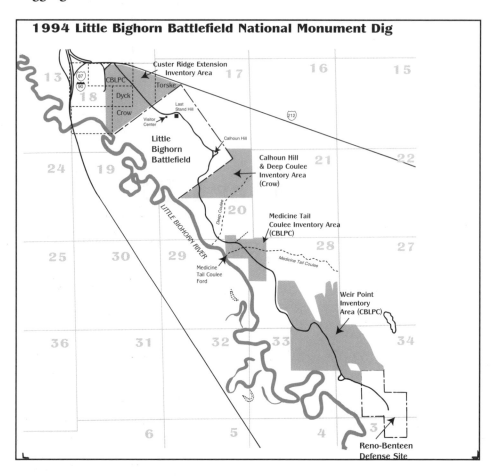

1994 Little Bighorn Battlefield National Monument Dig

The 1984 dig took place on the main battlefield and the 1985 work focused on the Reno-Benteen Defense Site. The 1994 dig covered privately owned acreage in the four shaded areas separate from the National Park Service sites.

(Map prepared by Gary Raham)

of Nebraska and Dick Harmon of the U.S. Geological Survey.

But the 1994 dig offered a profound difference from the major projects of earlier years. It would be the first to explore ground contested by the opposing sides in 1876 that lay outside the boundaries of the modern National Park Service administrative site.

Overlooking the Little Bighorn River southwest of Last Stand Hill
(Ralph Heinz)

Earlier digs had focused on government-held property on the main battlefield and at the Reno-Benteen Defense Site. In 1994, such privately held areas as Medicine Tail Coulee and Weir Point underwent formal archeological review. All in all, a total of 780 acres in four separate areas were inventoried during the project's two weeks.

First, on the northwest, a triangular plot of 295 acres was examined in an effort to ascertain as much as possible the northwest boundary of the actual battle. That land fell on both sides of the battlefield's entrance road, which begins at U.S. Highway 212, just about opposite the Custer Battlefield Trading Post. North of the entrance road, Highway 212 formed one edge of the area to be explored; on the other side of the entrance road, the search area reached into the valley itself, with a tip resting on the Little Bighorn River. The property belongs to several groups of owners. Some 40 acres adjacent to the entrance road are owned by Paul Dyck, who has long planned to construct a Plains Indian museum on his property to house his collection. Other segments are owned by local rancher Lynn Torske, the Custer Battlefield Land Preservation Committee (CBLPC) and the Crow tribe itself.

The NPS Resource Management Plan for the battlefield identified several thousand acres adjacent to the present park, including the 295 on the northwest, that ideally should be protected through cooperative management, easement or acquisition. According to Scott's 1994 dig report, "These lands are believed to have played a role in the battle as locations where Sioux and Cheyenne warriors fired upon the soldiers of the 7th Cavalry." This acreage took on added significance after the 1993 publication of Rich Fox's battle theory of a north movement by troops under Custer. Fox speculated that Custer and Companies E and F may have moved down the ridge from Last Stand Hill to the area outside the present park boundary in an attempt to reach a river ford north of the Indian camp along the Little Bighorn River. Either at the river or some early juncture, warriors blunted this maneuver and forced Custer to

Digging Into Custer's Last Stand

Dig volunteers searched Medicine Tail Coulee in 1994.

(Ralph Heinz)

retreat by a route that lies under the present-day government housing area, the historic Stone House and Custer Battlefield National Cemetery, and the NPS Visitors Center. Surviving soldiers regained Last Stand Hill, where Custer and remaining members of his command eventually were surrounded and wiped out.

While the government-held property has undergone significant development in this century, privately held and tribal acreage has largely avoided such intrusion. How long that can continue remains a matter of concern. Scott and Fox believed those lands might yield artifactual evidence of Custer's move to the river and the warriors' successful effort to force them back. On the other hand, Scott's report notes, "The 1994 inventory areas are known to have been metal detected and collected by a number of different individuals. Most detecting areas are unreported and most relic finds were not documented at the time of discovery. Many of these relics and activities cannot be documented further as many collectors are hostile to the National Park Service or fear legal retribution."

One effort to document such finds as reliably as possible was made by NPS historian Jerry Greene. He reported his efforts in his 1986 book, *Evidence and the Custer Enigma: A Reconstruction of Indian-Military History.*

The rationale for the 1994 dig project was in some ways as fortuitous as that for the 1980s' projects. Scott explains, "The issue had come up about doing an inventory of Paul Dyck's property. Rich had done a quick walkover of the site and had assessed the potential for having information. Obviously, there was some [artifacts] out there. [Park officials] began looking at the issue and realizing that Paul's land needed to be looked at."

Dyck was willing to allow his property to be searched and the Southwest Parks & Monument Association, which had succeeded the Custer Battlefield Historical & Museum Association as the auxiliary arm to the NPS, was willing to fund the work, which Scott expected could be done in a few days. About that time, battlefield historian Douglas McChristian realized "this was a good opportunity," Scott said. "Why not expand that project? So he talked to the Land Preservation folks [Harold Stanton and Jim Court] and got permission to look at their land."

McChristian realized, too, that the Torske and tribal lands were potentially valuable and the time might be at hand to do as much as possible, Scott explained. "There are areas we ought to be looking at to find out more about things."

So the concept of the 1994 dig expanded. On the battlefield's southeastern corner, beyond Calhoun Hill, lay some 155 acres of Crow tribal land. In the Medicine Tail Coulee vicinity another 160 acres are owned by the CBLPC. At Weir Point, that organization also held 250 acres, stretching on both sides of the prominent historic land feature. The final segment consisted of 20 acres the CBLPC held immediately adjacent to the Reno-Benteen area.

"Essentially, this project started out as a management issue dealing with Paul Dyck's land and then it blossomed," says Scott, adding that both the need and the opportunity for the field work were there. "This was a good way to check."

Scott and his team of professionals and volunteers spent two weeks con-ducting their investigations. During the inventory phase they relied on metal detectors, visual survey methods and piece-plot recording techniques, all similar to what was done in the 1980s. The metal detector operators aligned themselves at three to five meter intervals. They sought to walk a precise route while maintaining their intervals, but often rough terrain forced deviations.

Using hand tools, such as spades, trowels and dental picks, the recovery team carefully exposed an object's positioning in the ground as well as its specific location, as these were equal parts of the story it might tell the archeologists. According to Scott's report, "Artifacts were rarely found at depths that exceeded six inches."

As in earlier digs, recording data was important in 1994. Each artifact was assigned a sequential field-specimen number beginning at 8,000. While records were coded in a SDR33 data collector, Scott and company took no chances — a hand-written field-specimen catalog was also kept as a backup. The information was transferred daily from the SDR33 to a laptop computer.

The method of recording data was also similar to earlier projects. The recording instrument was set up at a known location on the ground, or datum point. Distance, azimuth and coordinate point readings for each artifact's location were recorded electronically. Its distance was read to the nearest millimeter as well as the north and east coordinate to the nearest second of a degree.

Once out of the ground, objects were cleaned by brushing and washing. Metallic items were treated in diluted glycolic acid to remove oxides built up during years in the ground. Each object was placed in a self-sealing clear plastic bag that bore its field specimen number and other identifying data. Eventually, the artifacts were shipped to the Midwest Archeological Center in Lincoln, Neb., for further study.

Given the combat situation inherent in the Little Bighorn, procedures for firearms analysis were again crucial. Scott repeated a familiar statement: "Firearms, in their discharge, leave behind distinctive metallic finger prints or signatures on the ammunition components. These signatures, called class characteristics, allow the determination of the types of firearm (i.e., model or brand) in which a given cartridge case or bullet was fired."

Continuing, Scott related how critical a comparison microscope is in analyzing bullets to see if they were fired from the same weapon. That instrument has two separate microscope tubes joined by a bridge with prisms mounted over the tubes. It transmits separate images to the center of the bridge where another set of prisms transmit the images to central eyepieces. The latter are divided so that each image

Digging Into Custer's Last Stand

Searching for artifacts northwest of Last Stand Hill in 1994.
(Ralph Heinz)

appears on one-half of each eyepiece. From such information, the number and the kinds of weapons can be determined and individual weapons can even be tracked across the battlefield.

According to Scott's report, "This capability is very important because coupled with the precise artifact locations, identical signatures can be used to identify specific combat areas. This can be done with cartridge cases and bullets even though actual weapons are not in hand. With this information, patterns of movement can be established and sequences of activity can be more precisely interpreted."

That last statement sums up a critical ingredient attesting to the value of the scientific investigations at the battlefield over the years. Scott considers the 1994 dig a success, although the number of artifacts collected during the two weeks — only about 320 — was much smaller compared to the earlier projects.

"We covered a lot of ground in that time, but [the number of artifacts] was very sparse in terms of artifact retrieval. But there was good information there. We would hit areas where large concentrations of material were and then be just dry as a bone elsewhere. I think that is indicative of what we were really dealing with — zones of combat occurring in there. That's where the debris got deposited. We also know the amount we recovered in any one place is nice. That probably reflects that people had previously collected in there, and we tried to assemble some of that information from disparate sources," such as long-time valley rancher Hank Weibert, his son Don

The terrain was more rugged south of Calhoun Hill, as the dig volunteers searched for artifacts.

(Ralph Heinz)

Weibert and NPS historian Jerry Greene, who formerly worked at Little Bighorn Battlefield National Monument.

"Combining the various sources, I think we get a much better picture of what some of those activities were," especially in the northwest where distribution of the relic data suggests some combatants used the ridge tops and ravines during the battle, Scott said in an interview.

"We got stuff just off or south of Calhoun, off toward Deep Coulee, which would indicate the two wings converging. To the north there were clusters of material, some army, and very definite evidence of what I perceived to be captured firearms that were used by the Indians because of the way they matched to some of the Calhoun stuff. So that's my interpretation of it. That does mean those weapons got from Calhoun to clear over to that north side. That's pretty remarkable."

His report summary offers several important conclusions of interest to students of the battle. In connection with the Weir Point movement by troops under Major Reno and Captain Benteen, he reports, "The archeological data confirm the Company D movement forward or north of Weir Point for approximately one-quarter mile. The firearms evidence indicates the line of the Company D retrograde movement to the Reno-Benteen defense site. This data, coupled with the 1985 archeological data on the retrograde movement, identifies that Company D covered the withdrawal from Weir Point to a position just west of the current monument fence."

In the Medicine Tail Coulee area, the archeological findings seem to support the present-day thinking of many who have studied the battle "that only a light action occurred at the ford." In addition, Scott concludes, "Some element of Custer's command, probably the left wing, moved from this action at the ford northeast up Deep Coulee to reunite with the right wing at or near Calhoun Hill. Battle debris found on this line as well as coming from Nye-Cartwright Ridge suggest the reunion movement was under fire and was contested."

He further states that firearms data and distribution patterns suggest the Indians moved into the Deep Coulee area after the soldiers gained Calhoun Hill. "The warriors were certainly on the right, left and front of the soldiers deployed at this southern end of the field." The evidence — army caliber bullets mixed with Indian caliber cartridge cases — also supports the notion that soldiers returned the warriors' fire.

Finally, Scott believes the archeological evidence supports the Fox theory of a 7th Cavalry movement to the north — that at least a portion of Custer's immediate command moved northwesterly along Custer Ridge before turning back or swinging over to Cemetery Ridge. However, the archeological project failed to yield data to support Fox's further belief that the 7th Cavalry made it to the river before being repulsed.

"Rich thinks they almost got to the river. I don't think they did," he explains. "They got a ways, but certainly not clear down to the river. The Cheyenne came across the river before Custer got halfway down there and pushed him back. That's where Rich and I would differ, but that's how I see the physical evidence."

He doesn't rule out the possibility that at least a few individuals, possibly some Army privates or newspaper reporter Mark Kellogg of the *Bismarck (Dakota*

Model 1870 Springfield
combination tool
(Ralph Heinz)

Curry comb
(Ralph Heinz)

Loaded .45-.55 carbine
cartridge found by Ralph Heinz
just north of the entrance station
to Little Bighorn Battlefield
National Monument.
(Ralph Heinz)

Territory) Tribune, made it to the vicinity of the river. "I can see Kellogg or someone else got popped down there," Scott says.

While the quantity of artifacts was small compared to earlier projects, the team did find a wide variety. "The majority of the specimens recovered can definitely be attributed to the battle while the remainder are mainly related to the post-battle era," Scott wrote in his report. "These latter artifacts primarily represent items related to Army visits to the site in years subsequent to the battle."

According to the report, the largest category of recovered artifacts, consistent with previous digs, includes bullets and cartridge cases, many of which are battle-related. One .30-caliber rimfire cartridge case was recovered in the Medicine Tail Coulee area. According to its firing pin mark, it may have been fired in a Remington-type revolver. This particular cartridge was designed for the Model 1 Remington-Smoot revolver introduced about 1873. Near Calhoun Hill, two types of distinctive Sharps bullets were found — a .40 caliber and a .50 caliber bullet.

During earlier projects, .44-caliber Henry rimfire cartridges and cartridge cases were commonly recovered items. That proved true again in 1994 as 14 cases were uncovered. The Henry Repeating Rifle was designed with a double firing pin that would strike the cartridge rim at separate points on either side. Two 1994 cases bear only a single firing pin mark, indicating they were fired from firearms other than the Henry chambered for the .44 caliber rimfire, the report says. One, Scott continues, was fired in the Colt Model 1871 Open Top Revolver and the other in a Ballard Sporting Rifle. Neither of these specimens matched firing pin imprints found in the earlier digs.

However, the other 12 cases that were fired in either a Henry Rifle or its improved version, the Model 1866 Winchester, demonstrated some matches. Two specimens, FS8018 and FS8019, were fired from the same weapon, while FS8208 and FS8209, were fired from another. FS8201 found in 1994 in the Calhoun area matches a 1984 artifact, FS375, that was recovered between the Keogh and Last Stand Hill areas. Another 1994 Calhoun area find, FS8252, matched four from 1994 and 1985 — three that were discovered in the Greasy Grass Ridge area and a fourth recovered near Sharpshooter Hill at the Reno-Benteen Defense Site. Scott concluded, "This match provides further support for the movement of warriors between the fields and movement around Custer battlefield."

Analysis of the double strike firing pin marks left on all the Henry .44-caliber cases and cartridges has identified 116 different Henry rifles and Winchester Model 1866s, Scott says. Of significance, three were used at both battlefields. Among bullets, 19 specimens from 1994 exhibit distinctive Winchester or Henry rifling marks. Because they are of the type used in the .44-caliber rimfire ammunition, not the earlier used .44/40-caliber center-fire ammunition, the archeologists concluded the majority were probably fired from either the Henry or Winchester Model 1866.

Two brass cartridge cases of .44/40 caliber found in the Weir Point area likely came from Model 1873 Winchester Repeating Rifles that were significantly improved over the Henry and Model 1866 because they could handle a heavier center-fire cartridge that could be reloaded. Analysis indicated these two cases were fired in different weapons. One, however, matched two cases found in the Calhoun

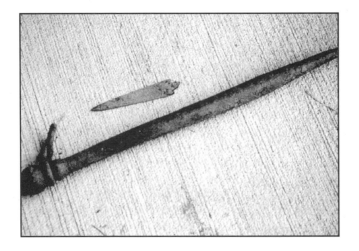

Arrowhead and picket pin recovered in 1994 were similar to objects found during the digs of the 1980s.
(Ralph Heinz)

Mess kit knife blade found in Medicine Tail Coulee
(Ralph Heinz)

1873 Springfield carbine trigger guard assembly and butt plate and tang screw
(Ralph Heinz)

area on Custer battlefield in earlier digs. This find provides more evidence of movement between sections of the combat arena by at least one warrior armed with a Model 1873 Winchester. The other 1994 find that did not match anything from earlier digs would add another model 1873 to the number identified, bringing that total to nine.

Another prominent weapon carried by 7th Cavalrymen was the .45-caliber Colt Single Action

Sharps paper patched bullet

(Ralph Heinz)

Army Revolver Model 1873 or possibly the .45 caliber Smith and Wesson Schofield revolver. Previously, 37 related cartridge cases had been found; in 1994, another eight surfaced, including seven in two small clusters in a ravine north of the battlefield's Visitors Center and just out of line of sight of Last Stand Hill. Another case was found below the modern park housing area.

According to analysis, the cases were fired in six different Colt revolvers. FS8049 and FS8950 matched each other as did FS8091 and FS8094. Both sets were within one to two meters of each other in the protected ravine. Scott theorized in his report that "This protected situation may be the reason these were deposited," adding that reloading the weapon takes time. "A location in a protected ravine and out of the line of fire, if the battle was still raging, would seem a likely scenario to fit the case find situation."

Interestingly, cases FS8049 and FS8050 matched a case, FS1605, found in Calhoun Coulee below Greasy Grass Ridge in 1984. The 1984 site is nearly one mile from 1994's.

Five .45-caliber bullets were uncovered in 1994. Four were found at the north end of the battlefield, while the fifth was adjacent to Calhoun Hill.

The principal firearm carried by the regiment at the battle was the Model 1873 Springfield carbine. Thirteen unfired .45/55-caliber cartridges for such a weapon were found in 1994, but two may represent post-battle ammunition. In addition, 49 fired cases and 93 .45/55 bullets were recovered. Five are considered post-battle items.

Firing pin and extractor mark examinations revealed 13 sets of matches of 1994 cases with those of 1984 and 1985. Intriguing interpretations arise from many of the matches. At least four cases found on the ridge north of Last Stand Hill matched earlier cases from Calhoun Hill more than a mile to the south. Six other guns are represented by the remaining cartridges, but their positioning indicates only minimal movement of the weapons. The cartridges found on the ridge in 1994 were intermixed with .44 Henry rimfire cases, Spencer rimfire cases and .50/70 centerfire cases representing Indian fired weapons.

Scott believes many of these weapons may represent pieces captured by the Indians and turned against the military.

"It's not like we had a bunch of Calhoun guys over there [on Last Stand Hill]. One or two escapees I could believe, or initial firing, but not likely to get that number of matches. So I believe what we are looking at are captured weapons that were employed against Custer," he said.

Initially, the team thought the material represented cavalry items, but, Scott said, "Then we started finding bunches of impacted .45 caliber bullets in and among these cartridge cases. That either means the Army was firing at the Army, or the Army was firing at a bunch of Indians who were there before or afterwards. My interpretation is that those are the captured carbines. Those are impacted army bullets in and among those cases probably fired from Last Stand Hill or that vicinity. The orientation of the impact is consistent with that, and, by the way, in the ravine you've got a superb line of sight up to Last Stand Hill."

Only two case examples, or about 4 percent, gave any evidence of extractor failure. That matched the rate of 1984 and 1985.

Fourteen cases, representing six Springfields, were found in the vicinity of Weir Point. Five cases were from the same gun that apparently moved from Weir Point toward the Reno-Benteen Defense Site. A second group of five cases were found with a single .50/70 case on the lower, or northeast, side of a small hillock several hundred yards north of Weir Point.

Another popular weapon of the period, the Spencer carbine, was produced in two calibers for both the civilian and military markets. Previously, eight cases were found on the main battlefield, and in 1994, three more were added. Two cases were used north of the Visitors Center. The third case came from near Weir Point. Two Spencer bullets were recovered during the search of Medicine Tail Coulee.

The .50/70 cartridge was developed for the army's service-wide adoption of a cartridge weapon and used by Springfield model rifles and carbines from 1866 to 1873. Various manufacturers, including Sharps and Remington, chambered single shot firearms for the .50/70 caliber. In 1994, eight .50/70-caliber cartridge cases and one .45/70 case fired in a .50/70-caliber gun were recovered. Firing pin analysis of the nine cases suggested they came from nine separate firearms — five Springfields, two Sharps and two Sharps or Remingtons — and boosted the total of .50/70-caliber weapons used in the battle to 57. None matched any previously discovered cases.

A few parts or tools of firearms were found in 1994. Two parts came from a .45 caliber Springfield carbine — a buttplate with inplace retaining screws and a trigger assembly with an associated broken tang retaining screw were found on a ridge top northwest of the housing area. Analysis suggested they could have been from a period weapon. In addition, a cylinder retention pin from a Colt Model 1873 revolver was found near the mouth of Medicine Tail Coulee where it enters the Little Bighorn River.

The fourth piece is a Model 1870 takedown tool and combination screwdriver found south of Weir Point. A standard Army issue tool used for disassembly and reassembly of weapons for field cleaning and repair, the item is a modified 1863 musket takedown tool originally intended for use with the Model 1866, 1868 and 1870 .50/70-caliber Springfield rifles. According to Scott's report, "Its presence near Weir Point suggests it was lost during the movements around that area, perhaps from a saddlebag of one of the soldiers during the retrograde movement from Weir Point to the Reno-Benteen Defense Site."

Since the digs began in 1984, 15 parts from firearms and one tool have been recovered by the archeologists. These earlier finds included:

- Five parts of a .50/70-caliber Springfield rifle, 1989
- Three carbine screws, 1985
- Ejector rod button for Colt pistol, 1984
- Colt Pistol backstrap, 1984
- Model 1858 Remington percussion revolver loading lever, 1984
- Percussion shotgun trigger, 1984, previously misidentified as a carbine trigger

Together, Scott believes, these individual parts represent at least 10 separate firearms.

OTHER ARTIFACTS RECOVERED IN 1994

Three knives: A generic-style, iron pocket knife with wooden handles that may or may not have been battle-related was one of three found during the dig. A standard 1874 pattern Army mess knife was found in two pieces near the mouth of Medicine Tail Coulee. The handle is broken near the blade tang but is all present, the report states. The blade is broken near the tip so its tip configuration could not be determined during studies. Finally, an iron skinning knife handle with brass rivets and washers was also found near the mouth of Medicine Tail Coulee. The blade is broken at the bolster. A plain 7/16 inch washer is on one side, while fancy washers with a human figure in the center appear on the other. The figure offers a full frontal view of an individual standing next to an anvil mounted on a base. According to the report, two similar but complete knives exist in private collections and feature a 10-inch iron or steel blade. One is marked on the blade "Martin Lutz, Solingen Prussia and Warranted by the Henry Sears Co. of Chicago." The other similar knife is unmarked except for the rivet washers.

Indian iron arrowheads: These have been found during previous digs, including eight arrowheads and one tip in 1984. Another one was found near Calhoun Hill in 1994. The report notes that these items were common trade pieces from the early 1600s to the early 20th century and had almost completely supplanted chipped stone projectiles by the mid-19th century. The 1994 specimen is similar to four others from 1984, having a straight tang with two barb-like protrusions midway on either side of the tang. The 3 1/2-inch long arrowhead is similar to one found in a human vertebra collected at Custer battlefield by the 1877 reburial party.

Clothing and personal items: Scott considers the seven items found in 1994 a small number. These included a finger ring, a brass bead, four buttons and fragments of a leather shoe or boot. In the past, rings have been artifacts to ponder, but the

1994 find proved less so. Made of brass and slightly crushed, it is large, measuring 3/4 inch in diameter and 1/3 inch in width. However, whether it was soldier- or Indian-related remains unclear, Scott says. "It's typical of the type that might have been a trade ring."

Miscellaneous items: These included two harness buckles, a brass D-buckle with an iron tongue found near Weir Point, and a buckle frame fragment found in Medicine Tail Coulee. The D-buckle was designed for a one-inch wide strap that was probably used on a horse nose feed bag. An iron ring of the type used in girthing was recovered on the flat below Cemetery Ridge. It is a non-military type that might have been either civilian or Indian. Also, a single link strap hook was recovered near Weir Point. Five horseshoes were found during 1994's dig, but whether they were battle-related could not be ascertained. Since 1876, horses have been used frequently in the battlefield area, but the construction and attachment of horseshoes have varied little during that time.

One complete Model 1859 army issue picket pin, similar to portions of four recovered from Reno-Benteen in 1985, was found near Calhoun Hill. It bears on the shank the name stamp, "O.B. North & Co.," a manufacturer of iron goods during the Civil War. In addition, parts of two pre-Civil War curry combs were recovered, one in a ravine below Last Stand Hill north of the Visitors Center and the other near Calhoun Hill.

WHAT WAS LEARNED FROM THE 1994 DIG?

Scott's report looks at the information for each of the project's areas of investigation separately, beginning with the Reno-Benteen and Weir Point episodes. He summarizes how Capt. Thomas Weir, commander of Company D, grew impatient as Major Reno and Captain Benteen hesitated on the bluffs to launch any attempt to link up with Custer. After Weir rode north toward present-day Weir Point, Lt. Winfield Edgerly, Company D's assistant company commander, mounted the men to follow Weir. After reaching Weir Point, Edgerly and the company ventured about another half-mile north. At either that point, or back at Weir Point, they exchanged shots with Indians some 150 to 200 yards in front of them.

Eventually, after the arrival of the pack train, Benteen with companies H, K and M, reached Captain Weir's position. Behind them, Reno and the remaining command sought to move the wounded forward. Soon the Indians began to flow south to challenge the soldiers still in the vicinity of Weir Point. The command was ordered to fall back to its original position on the bluffs, companies M and D covering the retrograde maneuver until a few hundred yards north of the modern Reno-Benteen site.

Near the present NPS northern fence line, Lt. Edward Godfrey organized Company K into a dismounted skirmish line to screen their retreating comrades. Only one man was lost during the retreat, the unfortunate farrier Vincent Charley, whose mutilated body was found after the battle. Soon, the entire command was under attack.

In his report for 1994, Scott concludes, "There is archeological evidence for the Weir Point episode that supports the statements made by the officers and men. In addition, the archeological data identifies the movement north of Weir Point, fighting around the Point, and the route of the retrograde movement back to the Reno-Benteen Defense Site. The archeological evidence is not extensive, but the data is patterned."

He points out that four .45/55 cases, all fired from the same gun, and one .50/70 and were found on the north side of a small knoll about one-fourth of a mile northeast of Weir Point. He concludes that at least two weapons fired from this location, and the artifacts were found below the crest of the knoll and protected from sight of Weir Point. According to his theory, the site might have been Edgerly's forward advance position, but "the evidence points to the strong possibility that this is an Indian position used to fire at the troops on Weir Point." None of these cases matched others collected during that year's project or earlier ones.

He points out that a .44-caliber rimfire case fired in a Henry or Model 1866 Winchester matched a case found at Calhoun Hill, indicating the weapon was used at two locations during the larger battle. Likewise, a .45/55 case (FS8518) found north of Weir Point matched four other cases — one (FS8517) found to the north, one (FS8503) near Weir Point, and two (FS8542, 8544) found west of Reno-Benteen and southwest of Sharpshooters Hill. "This group of cases fired from the same gun probably indicates the movement of one soldier," the report states. "These cases and their find locations are consistent with the Company D movement north of Weir Point, its movement back to Weir Point, and the subsequent retrograde movement back to Reno-Benteen."

An area in the valley owned by the Custer Battlefield Land Preservation Committee was examined to determine if it might be connected to an apparent village site discovered by rancher Jason Pitsch. His archeological efforts indicated a secondary Indian encampment might have existed there. It is believed to be where a band of about 20 warriors from the Spotted Tail Agency set up camp on the east side of the river near the upper end of the Indians' main village. However, the study of the CBLPC property yielded little data.

Besides the matched .45-caliber carbine case mentioned earlier, the area adjacent to the northwest fence corner of the Reno-Benteen Defense Site yielded only a few firearms-related items — two .45-caliber Springfield bullets, three additional .45/55 carbine cases and one .44-caliber Henry rimfire case. The area near the fence corner had been disturbed by earthmoving equipment when the park road was constructed. Still, objects found near the fence and south of Sharpshooters Hill suggest the troops passed over the site while retreating from Weir Point. Later, warriors may have fired on the troops from there.

The inquiry in Medicine Tail Coulee developed what the report describes as "meager" archeological evidence of combat at the mouth of the coulee. Blame is placed on previous artifact collecting and other uses of the land, including grazing. It further notes that "ample evidence" of the making of the 1970 movie, "Little Big Man," was recovered in the vicinity, including on a cut bank east of the tour road at the mouth of Deep Coulee, where the Last Stand sequence itself was filmed.

Digging Into Custer's Last Stand

Additional movie debris from the filming of the charge to the river at the mouth of Medicine Tail Coulee where it joins the Little Bighorn River was recovered in that area.

The report finds it interesting that "the locations used in the movie to represent battle sequences were in fact set on sites actually used in the battle." The area along the tour road where the Last Stand was filmed yielded lead balls and Sharps bullets believed fired by warriors and a .45-caliber carbine bullet fired by a soldier. "These data alone indicate there was combat in this area," according to the report. Further, the Indian bullets impacted on the east side of Deep Coulee "may represent shots fired in the direction of retreating soldiers or they may represent shots fired at Yates' wing as they moved to the mouth of the coulee in their movement toward the river."

Citing previous work by historians Don Rickey and J.W. Vaughn and noting that a few objects were found in 1994, the report concludes that the data supports the historical record's contention that "a small action with only limited firing occurred at the ford." The objects found in 1994 were two pieces of a broken Model 1874 army mess knife, a period butcher knife that might have been civilian or Indian, a lead rifle ball and the cylinder pin to a Colt revolver.

The Calhoun Hill area inquiry occurred in the upper portion of Deep Coulee adjacent to the park's southeastern corner and yielded 88 items, most of which were bullets and cartridge cases. These included:

- 2 .45-caliber Army cartridges
- 4 unfired cartridges
- 28 .45 caliber bullets
- 8 .44-caliber rimfire cases
- 5 .44-caliber bullets
- 4 cartridges cases and 2 cartridges in .50/70-caliber
- 11 .50-caliber bullets
- 1 .40-caliber Sharps bullet
- 1 lead ball
- 2 .50-caliber bullets fired in different Sharps Sporting rifles
- 2 brass spurs (1 a regulation spur and the other an earlier
     Army model)
- 1 picket pin
- 1 curry comb
- 1 iron arrowhead
- 1 iron awl

One of the .44-caliber rimfire cases matched a case found in 1985 at the Reno-Benteen Defense Site, providing evidence that the Henry or Model 1866 Winchester was used at both battlefields. Scott concludes, "The artifact patterning and distribution gives the impression of soldiers moving up Deep Coulee toward Calhoun Hill. The expended Army cartridge case distribution indicates there was some firing as the movement took place, but it appears light or at least limited in scope."

The report continues: "The distribution of Indian caliber bullets also gives the distinct impression that the Army movement was under fire. Most Army bullets were found around the park's boundary fence near Calhoun Hill. The same is true of most of the Indian caliber cartridge cases."

Scott concludes, "Most of these bullets were deposited as a result of firing by Companies C and L after their deployment at the south end of Custer or Battle Ridge." As some Army caliber bullets were also found northeast of the fence corner, apparently fired at warriors in the area of Henry Ridge, he speculates one of these Indians may have been Gall, who "stated he joined the battle at Calhoun Hill via a route through Henry Ridge."

All in all, Scott believes the 1994 dig not only met its goals but also contributed still more data that will prove important to future researchers and historians trying to unravel the mysteries of what happened and how at the Battle of Little Bighorn. For one, while the numerical count in artifacts discovered was relatively small, the team did find material in each of the inventoried areas and it was in recognizable patterns. The cartridge cases and bullets recovered again were significant as these latest items continued to broaden the understanding of weapons used at the battle by both sides. Two new types of firearms — the Ball carbine and the Remington-Smoot .30-caliber rimfire revolver — brought the total of identified firearms types to 47. In addition, lab studies of individual characteristics of bullets and firing imprints on cartridge cases added 41 individual firearms, bringing the total known to have been used by one or both sides to 413. The additional 41 in 1994 included:

- 5 Colt Model 1873 revolvers
- 12 Model 1873 Springfield carbines
- 5 .50/70 Springfields
- 2 Sharps
- 2 Sharps or Remington rifles
- 1 Model 1872 Open Top Colt Revolver
- 2 Spencer carbines
- 1 Ball carbine
- 1 Remington-Smoot revolver
- 2 Model 1873 Winchester rifles or carbines
- 8 .44-caliber rimfire Henry or Model 1866 Winchester rifles

Scott thinks the data not only yielded new information but also support the historical record and Native American oral testimony about both combatant movements and actions in each of the locales. For example, the archeological data confirm that Company D moved to the front of Weir Point, or north, for about a quarter mile. The company's trek back from Weir Point can also be traced through the firearms evidence. When viewed in conjunction with data from 1985, that company can be seen as having maintained its role in the retrograde operation until it reached a point just west of the current NPS boundary fence at Reno-Benteen.

While the new data from the Medicine Tail Coulee area were rather minuscule compared to other areas, Scott believes it, too, is important. It supports the historical contention that only "light action" occurred between whatever elements of the 7th Cavalry approached the river ford from the east and the Indian combatants in the village on the valley side. Perhaps of greater importance, what was learned supports the belief of historians, as Scott's report indicates, "that some element of Custer's command, probably the left wing, moved from this action at the ford northeast up Deep Coulee to reunite with the right wing at or near Calhoun Hill. Battle debris found on this line as well as coming from Nye-Cartwright Ridge suggest the reunion movement was under fire and was contested."

The report further concludes: "The archeological firearms data and distribution patterns indicate the warriors took possession of this terrain after the soldiers deployed on and near Calhoun Hill." As the soldiers were deployed, they faced warriors on their right, left and front, but were active in contesting with fire the movement of their opponents, as indicated by the discovery of Army bullets mixed with Indian caliber cartridge cases in this area.

For students of the battle, evidence of the probable movement north by Custer's own command along the extensions of Custer Ridge and Cemetery Ridge is also important. "The archeological data indicate Custer and the left wing may have moved northwesterly along Custer Ridge before turning back or swinging over to Cemetery Ridge," the report states.

After halting Custer's advance and forcing him back to what would become the scene of the last stand by the army — or at least by one group of Custer's total command — the warriors used several positions to fire at the soldiers in their defensive position. "Many of those warriors were using captured Army weapons, some definitely captured from the right wing dead at Calhoun Hill and Calhoun Coulee. The soldiers on Last Stand Hill were not idle and returned fire until they were finally overrun," he says. Scott does not maintain that these soldiers were the last to fall on the field, but clearly he believes a strong engagement occurred before the 45 or 50 men found there were killed.

SCOTT LOOKS BACK AT THE DIGS

More than 14 years after the opening event that literally sparked the archeological searches at Custer/Little Bighorn Battlefield National Monument, Doug Scott looks back with both a sense of pride as well as amazement at all the digs have meant to the continuing efforts to unravel the mysteries of the Montana battle.

"I am very pleased that the work we did was well-received by the public, and for the most part, most of the Custer-Little Bighorn researcher crowd," Scott said in an interview. "But what I feel is probably most important is that the park staff and others have picked up the information we have presented, and they have used it in their interpretation. In other words, they have integrated history and archeology and ethno-history — telling a more complete story to the public."

He added that even critics of the projects acknowledge that "the archeology is now a part of that [interpretation] as a routine." The continuing interest in the battlefield work stands in sharp contrast to the common reaction to most archeological projects. Usually, the field work is completed, reports are written, but nothing of immediate value to the public results. However, reaction to the work at Little Bighorn Battlefield Monument has been different.

"The whole issue of interpretation in that park and to the public is now an integrated, multi-disciplinary approach to things," he says. "It's not just history or one person's opinion. The interpreters, when they go in to learn about how to give talks, have to read something about the archeology and the ethno-history. I think that well-rounded approach is really good."

When Fox and he began their work after the fire of 1983, they figured they, too, would complete their work and move on to other tasks. "In many ways both of us have done that [but] certainly that [battlefield project] has enhanced our careers," he acknowledges. Still, they are proud, he said, that "Within our profession there's a level of recognition for having done some pretty innovative research and applied some methodology that has now become standard within historical archeology — the application of metal detectors."

But he finds another more important dimension to the continuing long-term focus on the digs. "I think the other level that neither of us probably envisioned — may have hoped for, but probably never envisioned — was the abiding interest that has continued in the recovery of information from an archeological context. There are so many people interested in the Little Bighorn story and always the thirst for new information. Well, some of that new information is only available with physical evidence."

He specifically cited writings by Richard Hardorff, Gregory Michno, James S. Brust and this author that have integrated newly discovered or newly interpreted information from the historical record with archeological evidence. "I think it's one of those things that we should have recognized earlier on," he said. "Nobody is ever going to hold all the cards and be able to tell the whole story. There is always that new diary that shows up or there is that new photograph, or there is another piece of physical evidence that happens to show up that has eroded out that we didn't see before."

For himself, he thinks the review of one set of human remains that were exhumed from the National Cemetery and determined to be those of farrier Vincent Charley, killed on the Weir Point retreat, underscores how important blending the findings of archeology with historical records is.

"Now we know about him. We know he had a busted arm at one point and a busted rib, and somebody stomped on his foot, or something had stomped on his foot. All of that is very consistent with being a blacksmith and a farrier. Not to say that's how all that happened, but you can certainly see that he was a very robust, heavily muscled individual, the proverbial blacksmith under the spreading chestnut tree. To me, that helps tell that story a little better. I can see that guy now. He's not just some blue-clad cavalryman riding off into the sunset. I can see somebody, and the facial reconstruction helps that, of course. The interpreters can weave quite a story out of that."

He finds the Little Bighorn unique in what it offers both the professional historian and the popular buff. The scope of the action actually enables a big picture approach to the military engagement itself as well as a more individual focus on the men of either side who fought there. "The story of the Little Bighorn is really the story of those people. Where else do we have the opportunity to look at the individuals, not the officers, not the commanders, but the average guy who is out there?" Not only the John Ryans or Mark Kelloggs, but also such men as Daniel Kanipe or Mike Madden. The latter was wounded at Reno-Benteen while defending the men descending Water Carriers Ravine and his leg had to be amputated.

"What about Mike Madden?" he asks. "We don't know much about him after he left the service and he disappears from the historical record in the 1880s. Where is he? There was a colorful character who had a great story. I can see this guy gimping around, kicking open the swinging doors to a bar in downtown St. Louis, crutching his way in or peglegging his way in, caging drinks and telling stories about the Little Bighorn."

He added, "I find it personally much more interesting to deal at the individual level. How does this person fit into the Army, how does he fit into his company, how does he react? What are his opinions? Those are the people who were out there on the line doing the fighting."

After 14 years of archeological inquiries at Little Bighorn, he doesn't foresee an end any time soon. For one thing, at any park, and Little Bighorn is no exception, maintenance or construction work often requires new efforts. For example, at some point the site of the planned Indian Memorial at the battlefield will require research before construction begins.

Large-scale projects are another question. "There are always new questions that we can come up with based on analysis of what we've done or areas of investigation. At some point in principle I suppose we can exhaust all possibilities, but I doubt it."

One project that may not be accomplished for a long time concerns the enduring mystery of Deep Ravine and 28 men of Company E who may have died there. In the summer of 1996, tests were conducted by ground-penetrating radar and magnetometry, modern technology that sends electronic pulses, either radar, magnetic or electrical, into the earth. Scott explained that such tests "will discover things that are not normal or indicate changes in soil type. These are commonly used techniques in geophysics to locate oil fields or mineral-bearing rocks for mining."

He added, "It's not an untried technology, but it's new at the scale we're doing, it to adapt it for finding real small things," such as land mines, especially made of plastic. The Little Bighorn Battlefield became a place to fine tune the technology in what he labeled as "a demonstration technology situation."

When the news broke in the fall of 1996 that the tests had discovered "an anomaly" in the ravine's soil, many overeager buffs incorrectly concluded the whereabouts of the remains of the 7th Cavalrymen who died there had been revealed. Scott downplays such expectations, noting specifically the equipment "won't find bones. They might find a mass of artifacts together," but more likely will indicate changes in soil, such as where a pit may have been dug or soil filled in.

"At this point, it could be nothing more than a natural change of soil," he emphasized, "but it will give us some place to focus on for the future. I'm more encouraged by this anomaly because we have a place to look. It gives us more ammunition to decide where to look and how to handle (the project)."

Still, NPS officials, remain understandably cool to the idea of digging up the ravine to see what, if anything, may be there. Scott supports that view. "For the moment, there is not a compelling reason to dig in the ravine," he explained. "It would do more damage there than may be warranted."

Resources for conducting such a project would dwarf what has been needed for all the previous work on the battlefield, including earthmoving equipment and hydraulic shoring mandated by the usually high water table in the ravine. He pegs the cost of such an effort at between $150,000-$250,000, an imposing obstacle compared to earlier projects.

"That cost is too high, especially considering the resource damage that would occur," he said, adding, "We do not need to know [what is there] at this point." That is, the ravine itself would be irrevocably altered by the project. He doesn't think the potential knowledge to be gained warrants virtually destroying the Deep Ravine. Instead, he is optimistic that promising technologies might make a future archeological effort cheaper and less invasive.

So for the time being the battlefield will continue to conceal one of its more tantalizing mysteries, but Scott thinks other projects may yet be conducted seeking to answer the lingering questions. "I don't think anything like this [archeology] ever has a complete closure. We can stop. I can stop at any point here and say, 'Well, I am done. I'm not going to do anything more at the Little Bighorn," he said, "although I don't think that will likely be happening in the next few years."

Chapter Eight

HUMAN REMAINS ON

LITTLE BIGHORN BATTLEFIELD

"Oh, What tales bones could tell — and often do!"

In the 1991 *Greasy Grass* magazine, that sentence appeared as the headline over an article by Doug Scott and Douglas Owsley, who had examined the skeletal remains of several soldiers either seriously wounded or killed during the Battle of Little Bighorn. In the beginning of their article, the two experts noted that across the decades the battlefield has yielded bones of many men who were killed either June 25 or June 26, 1876. Not counting formal archeological efforts, some 20 discoveries of human bone have been documented since 1877. In a few cases, nearly complete skeletons were found and reburied. More often, body parts — perhaps an arm, leg, foot or hand — were found exposed on the surface of the ground. During the archeological investigations of 1984 and 1985, the fragmentary remains of 34 soldiers who died with Custer were uncovered. The historical record makes clear that in the early years after the fighting, visitors to the battlefield could see the literal remains of the men who had been given at best cursory burials. Oftentimes, these bones were claimed as souvenirs. Only occasionally were they provided to experts to be preserved in the battlefield's museum collection or some other repository.

As Scott and Owsley stated in their article, "Until recently no systematic effort to identify or study these remains or determine what the bones could tell us had been conducted. The battlefield archeological projects of the 1980s provided the opportunity to study the bones and develop an osteobiography of each of the men represented." In addition, Scott has led efforts to locate other bones related to the Battle of the Little Bighorn and to continue to develop an osteobiographic profile of the men who died with Custer. Most notably, this involved in 1992 the exhumation of seven graves in the Custer Battlefield National Cemetery that held the remains of 10 individuals, including one who proved to be a Native American.

Out of all of these studies, conducted since the beginning of the archeological projects more than a decade ago, have come important details about the diet, health, diseases, injuries and manner of death of men of the 7th U.S. Cavalry. Not only has this work resulted in the creation of a substantial database of new information about the 7th Cavalry's troopers, but it also has led to matching up four sets of remains with the names of specific individuals — Sgt. Edward Botzer, Sgt. Miles O'Hara, interpreter Mitch Boyer and Farrier Vincent Charley. A fifth set of remains was earlier identified as those of Corp. George Lell by Scott and his forensic experts. Based on their earlier reports, we included information about Lell's apparent identification in the 1998 edition of this book. However, further DNA testing by forensic personnel has led them to a new determination that the remains were not Lell's. Their new information will be included later in this chapter.

(James Woodcock, Billings, Mont., Gazette)

Public interest in the projects, of course, has focused on what the digs could reveal about the tide of battle. But just as often, the public's and the news media's attention has dwelled on the search for remains — especially on remains actually located. Perhaps the best example of that, as noted in Chapter 3 on the 1989 dig, occurred while veteran Hollywood producer Bill Armstrong had a crew at the battlefield during that project shooting a documentary later broadcast on the Arts & Entertainment Network under the catchy title of "Custer's Last Trooper." On the day in May 1989 that Monte Kloberdanz found a human skull, humerus and clavicle in the roots of a cottonwood tree along the riverbank at the Reno Retreat Crossing, Armstrong realized he had a more exciting focus for his documentary than the mere search of a presumed cavalry dump site.

"Custer's Last Trooper" — facial reconstruction done by Betty Pat Gatliff
(Bill Armstrong)

Armstrong recalled that "Harness rivets, supply box parts and saddle staples kept the volunteer crews at high intensity, but the muttered prayer of 'please, just one lousy carbine barrel' became a daily litany — but the various gods invoked were not of a giving vein."

But with the discovery of the skull, Armstrong said, "There was an electric excitement among the volunteers — a real find! While certainly not part of the survey, the find was significant and boosted the morale of the volunteers — and quickly changed the title of the documentary from 'Lost Treasures of the Little Big Horn' to 'Custer's Last Trooper'."

Using information about the soldier's physical description, the archeological team narrowed his identity to two highly probable candidates — Sgt. Edward Botzer, Company G, and Pvt. William Moodie (Moody), Company A. In 1989, forensic sculptress Betty Pat Gatliff had completed a cast and a facial reconstruction of the skull, which were featured in Armstrong's television special, "Custer's Last Trooper." She prepared a clay model built up over the skull. Various "landmarks" on the skull served as guides for the sculptor about how the person might have looked in life. Through her training and skill, she determined the size of the mouth, the shape of the nose, and the placement of the ears and eyes by reading the indicators on the skull itself. What resulted was a remarkable likeness of the person. However, in this instance the lack of any previously known photos of Botzer and Moodie to compare to the skull or to Gatliff's reconstruction stymied efforts to identify the soldier. The remains themselves were later reburied in Custer Battlefield National Cemetery.

Still, speculation for several years focused on Botzer, in part because of an

Individual believed to be Sgt. Edward Botzer
(Hayes Otoupalik and Brad Dahlquist)

account by Pvt. Augustus DeVoto that indicated the sergeant's corpse had been among those identified at the river crossing. According to the historical record, Botzer was killed June 25, 1876, at the ford when the Reno battalion retreated from the valley. Born in Bremerhaven, Germany, Botzer enlisted at age 26 or 28 for the second time in the 7th U.S. Cavalry on Nov. 26, 1871, at Spartanburg, S.C. On the day he was killed, Botzer would have been between 30 to 34. He had blue eyes, brown hair and a fair complexion, and stood 5'6 1/2".

Finally, in 1995, Brad Dahlquist contacted me to offer a series of photos from his collection for possible publication in *Greasy Grass* magazine. One image he believed to be Botzer. Dahlquist had obtained the original from an antique dealer. A pencil inscription on the back of the photo says, "Sgt. Edward Botzer killed with Col. Custer."

In an effort to confirm Botzer's identity and put a name with the skull from the Reno Crossing, I sent copies of the full-figure photograph of the soldier to Scott and battlefield historian Doug McChristian. Forensic anthropologist P. Willey of Chico State University in Chico, Calif., and Richard Vertolli of the Chico State Instructional Media Center used video cameras, a monitor and a dissolve unit to superimpose the facial image of the soldier in the photograph over that of an exact cast of the original skull, since reburied in the Custer Battlefield National Cemetery. As we will see, similar techniques led to identification of several other military victims of the Little Bighorn, notably scout Mitch Boyer and Sgt. Miles O'Hara.

Results of tests on the Botzer photo weren't quite as conclusive as the experts would have liked. Unfortunately, the skull's lower jaw bone was missing, meaning they could not compare important features of the face. "The (Botzer) image is not as exact or positive as we would have hoped," Willey said, but he added, "Generally we found the features of the skull fit the photograph,"

He concluded, "The best we can say is that we can't exclude the possibility that the photo is the same person. I don't see anything that would rule it out and it remains a viable possibility."

Scott, while agreeing with Willey, stressed that the video testing of the Botzer image certainly provided further weight to the prevailing theory that the German native was likely the soldier whose skull was recovered in 1989. "We can't say absolutely that it's Botzer, but we can't say it isn't. All the circumstantial evidence certainly points in that direction (to Botzer)."

Battlefield historian McChristian also studied the Botzer photo. In researching and clarifying the previously published historical record of Botzer, he dated the photo to 1870-72, based on the soldier's uniform. However, the soldier's Spencer carbine raised some doubt for McChristian, who pointed out that the 7th Cavalry turned in its Spencers prior to January 1871. Also, the man appears to be wearing a wedding ring, but Botzer, as far as was known, was single.

Scott strongly leans toward the identification of the remains as Botzer's. He notes, "We probably never can exclude Moodie until we have a photo of him that also can be tested."

INTERPRETER MITCH BOYER

Among the personalities who fought at the Little Bighorn with the Army, none appears more intriguing than interpreter and scout Mitch Boyer (Bouyer). His mother was a full Santee Sioux and his father, Vital Bouyer, was a French Canadian blacksmith who was killed by Indians while trapping near Fort Laramie in Wyoming. During the 1876 campaign, Mitch Boyer worked as an interpreter for the Crow Scouts attached to the 7th Cavalry on June 22. Early on the morning of June 25, he went to the Crow's Nest with Lt. Charles Varnum. At the time he was believed to be between age 35 to 40. That afternoon he accompanied the Custer battalion and died. Where he was killed has never been fully settled by the historical record. One account said his body was never found; another said his body was seen in the Little Bighorn River and was identified by a calf-skin vest it wore. Other accounts placed Boyer on Last Stand Hill, in Deep Ravine, or halfway between the Custer field and the Reno-Benteen site four miles south.

Mitch Boyer
(Little Bighorn Battlefield National Monument)

After identification of partial remains found at this site as Boyer's, his name was added to the marker.
(Sandy Barnard)

Enter archeology. After the battlefield fire in the summer of 1983, archeologist Richard Fox discovered human bone eroding from the ground adjacent to Markers 33 and 34 along the Deep Ravine Trail. The next year, the site near the crest of a small ridge about halfway between Deep Ravine and today's visitors center received a more detailed archeological survey. A number of interesting objects were retrieved: a few river cobbles, a .50/70 bullet, a lead shot, a rubber button, three trouser buttons and a shank type mother-of-pearl shirt button.

More important, bone material in the excavation pit included skull fragments, a finger and the tail bone. Forensic study suggested the teeth

Digging Into Custer's Last Stand

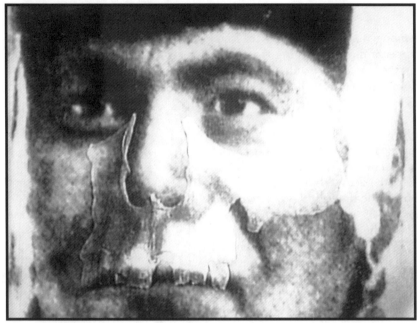

This match of the facial bones with the known photo of Mitch Boyer would stand up in a court of law, according to forensic experts.

(Little Bighorn Battlefield National Monument)

were worn in a pattern familiar to a pipe smoker's and appeared to be curved and shovel-like, similar to the backs of teeth of American Indians. The individual was clearly a male, likely between 35-40, and his head had apparently been struck by a heavy blunt instrument, sustaining massive blunt force trauma about the time of death. Most important, his racial heritage appeared to be a Caucasian/Mongoloid admixture.

As Scott and co-authors Melissa Connor and Clyde Snow wrote in a 1988 *Greasy Grass* article, "At this point the forensic data suggested a unique individual. The face bones suggested the man was part-Indian. The mother-of-pearl button suggested he wore Euro-American, but not Army regulation, clothing." His place of death was along the traditional soldier line of battle called the South Skirmish Line.

"The data suggested he was a part-Indian civilian, fighting with Custer's troops. The only person that fit this description was Mitch Boyer, a 38-year-old half-Indian scout." Boyer, too, was known to be a pipe smoker.

To verify Boyer's identification, Scott and his associates relied on a forensic identification technique that would prove useful in this instance as well as in later cases, such as Botzer's — superimposing images of the skull bone with a photograph of the individual in question. The facial bones used consisted of the left side of the cheek, a partial left eye orbit, and the front teeth and nasal cavity. "The match of the orbit with the eye, the nasal cavity with the nose and the teeth with the mouth was exact, and in all probability, indicate the remains are Boyer's," the authors wrote.

At the time renown forensic anthropologist Clyde Snow believed he could prove Boyer's identity "in a court of law."

The team of experts suggested there was only one chance in a hundred the individual was not Boyer. Adding to the probability of a match was Boyer's status as the only individual of a racially mixed heritage accompanying Custer's immediate command. Boyer's remains were among those reburied in the National Cemetery in June 1986.

SGT. MILES O HARA

With all the excitement engendered by the string of archeological projects, many students of the battle overlook an earlier project conducted in 1958 by Robert Bray at the Reno-Benteen Defense Site prior to the construction of the present battlefield road. Three sets of soldier remains were uncovered by Bray and studied in the mid-1980s by Scott's team. They were later reburied in June 1986. Forensic study of one set of remains indicated they were Sgt. Miles O'Hara, Company M. The remains, consisting of a skull, left arm, a rib and two vertebrae, indicated the soldier was between ages 25 and 27, stood 5'8" and had a light to medium build. Betty Pat Gatliff completed a facial reconstruction of the skull. O'Hara's military records matched up nicely with the forensic data and a known picture of him seemed to resemble the Gatliff facial reconstruction. Scott concluded, "The forensic and physical data make O'Hara a definite candidate for the identity" of the 1958 Bray project remains.

Unfortunately, in this instance archeology raised as many new questions as it answered. In O'Hara's case, and to a lesser extent, in Boyer's, the archeological

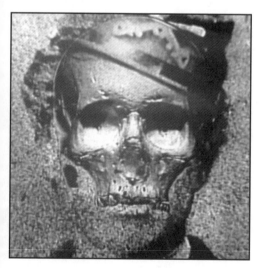

Skull from the L-entrenchment at Reno-Benteen shows exact fit with a known photograph of O'Hara.
(Little Bighorn Battlefield National Monument)

locations don't line up well with the historical record. An account by First Sgt. John Ryan of Company M as well as interviews of Privates Roman Rutten and James Wilber by researcher Walter Mason Camp clearly placed O'Hara's death site on the Reno skirmish line in the valley, not up on the bluffs in an entrenchment in the area of Company H. Pvt. Edward Pigford told Camp that O'Hara was shot on the line, but actually was killed attempting to retreat into the timber. While the archeologists speculated his body might have been recovered after the fighting ended or the wounded O'Hara somehow made it to the top of the bluffs only to die later in the make-shift hospital, the historic record provides no information about such events.

Forensic sculptor Betty Pat Gatliff reconstructed this face on the skull recovered in 1958 from the L-entrenchment at Reno-Benteen. The resemblance to Miles O'Hara is considered strong by the experts.
(Little Bighorn Battlefield National Monument)

CORP. GEORGE LELL

In May 1992, the National Park Service agreed to let Scott excavate seven graves in the Custer Battlefield National Cemetery containing 10 remains of unknowns recovered earlier in this century. According to cemetery records, five graves dated to 1903. A sixth was created in 1928 and involved two separate burials. The seventh's date of interment was unclear and could only be categorized as pre-1940.

In 1903, battlefield Supt. A.N. Grover had visited the Reno-Benteen site, accompanied by battle survivor and Medal of Honor winner Henry W.B. Mecklin. They opened several graves on the battlefield and the skeletons were transferred to five graves in the National Cemetery. The headstones placed on the graves were marked "Unknown" or "Unknown U.S. Soldier," although the skeletons as a group were attributed to Farrier Vincent Charley, Company D; Corp. George Lell Company H; Pvt. Thomas Meador, Company H; Pvt. James Tanner, Company M; and Pvt. Henry C. Voight, Company M. Charley was reportedly found in a swale between Weir Point and Sharpshooter Ridge, while the other four were uncovered in one grave on Reno Hill. At the time no specific individual identity was attached to any of the five graves.

After exhumation in 1992 by Scott and his co-workers, the skeletons underwent osteological analysis to confirm their identity as 7th Cavalrymen and to gather further details about their lives and manner of death. The skeletons were taken initially to the Midwest Archeological Center, Lincoln, Neb., for cleaning and then were forwarded to Chico State University, Chico, Calif., where forensic anthropologist P. Willey analyzed them. His conclusions at that time supported two of the identifications as Lell and Charley.

Lell was born in Hamilton County, Ohio, about 1847. At age 14, he appeared in the 1860 census for Green Township in rural Hamilton County, living with his father, also named George, and his mother, Ann, both of whom were born in Bavaria. All of young George's siblings (four sisters and one brother) were born in this country.

Young George was enlisted in nearby Cincinnati by Lt. Adam Kramer on Sept. 18, 1873. According to his enlistment record, he was 26 years, stood 5 feet 9 inches tall, with blue eyes, and dark hair and complexion. A photo of Lell indicates he was a handsome young man. In civilian life, he had been a gas fitter. With the 7th Cavalry, he was assigned to Company H and eventually promoted to corporal. During the first day of the battle he fought in the valley and on the Reno-Benteen hilltop. On the second day, June 26, he was wounded by a bullet in the abdomen. Taken to the hospital area, he died either that day or the following day. His death was recalled by Pvt. Charles A. Windolph:

"He was dying and knew it. 'Lift me up, boys,' he said to some of the men. 'I want to see the boys again before I go.' So they held him up to a sitting position where he could see his comrades in action. A smile came to his face as he saw the beautiful fight the 7th was making. They laid him down and he died soon after."

His body was buried in a grave with the bodies of Privates Meador, Tanner and Voight, although one account suggests Tanner and Voight were buried in a separate grave. The grave was in the hilltop siege area, most likely one of the trenches or holes used in the defense. In 1903, he was removed for reburial in National Cemetery Grave 453; Scott designated his remains as Burial 2.

According to analysis, this skeleton was fairly well preserved with most elements present. As reported in *Greasy Grass* magazine in 1996, "The skeleton was of a gracile white male, 30-35 years old and 5 feet 5.3 inches tall. A few minor skeletal injuries were discovered. Degenerative changes (arthritis) of the jaw may have been caused by his grinding of his teeth during sleep (bruxism). The spine also displayed degeneration, indicating a bad back." Surprisingly, the remains gave no indication of what caused his death.

What most interested the experts were the individual's teeth. As Scott said, this man "had relatively good oral health." He had all his teeth at the time of death (although some were subsequently lost, most likely during the original exhumation and transportation to the National Cemetery), unlike the other men whose teeth were either in poor condition or missing. The teeth of the man designated as Burial 2 had stains consistent with tobacco consumption. Wear on the teeth suggested the tobacco may have been consumed as "chaw."

Also of interest were at least six fillings in the molars, four in the upper jaw and two in the lower. According to the *Greasy Grass* article, "Four of the fillings were gold and two were tin. Two of the gold fillings were in the tiny, naturally occurring pits on the sides of the lower teeth, suggesting a very special dentistry setting, such as a teaching situation, or a relative or friend who was a dentist. In addition to these fillings, two other locations likely had been filled, but the fillings were subsequently lost."

Once again, Betty Pat Gatliff sculpted a facial approximation for comparison to known photos. Eight men emerged as possibilities for the identity of the man in Grave 453, Burial 2 skeleton, but the experts wrote that Lell provided the best match: "Lell's enlistment record, historic accounts and a photograph compare favorably with the skeletal determinations. Lell was about 29 years old at the time of the battle and the skeleton was 30-35 years old. Lell was struck in the abdomen, which, depending on the exact location of the bullet's entrance and trajectory, may not have left any marks on the skeleton. The bones showed none. Lell's remains were said to have been among those recovered and moved to the National Cemetery in 1903. The skeleton was buried in the cemetery in 1903. And when the skull and Lell's photograph were superimposed, the contours and the proportions fit. All of these characteristics support the identification."

Also noteworthy, Lell came from southwestern Ohio, near Cincinnati, where the Ohio College of Dental Surgery was established in 1848 as the world's second dental college. Lell could have been treated there or by one of several well-trained dentists in the area, but, unfortunately, no records indicate he ever was a patient there.

In the effort to match the skeleton to Lell, one problem arose. Lell reportedly was 5 feet 9 inches but the skeletal height was 5 feet 5.3 inches, a difference of more than three inches. Possibly the individual's height was incorrectly recorded or measured during enlistment. Despite the stature discrepancy, the study concluded, "It is likely that Grave 453, Burial 2 is the skeleton of George Lell."

Alas, Willey's initial optimism about this possible identification of Lell has proved to be incorrect in the longer run, thanks to modern scientific use of DNA.[1] Since its establishment in 1976, the U.S. Army's Central Identification Laboratory in Hawaii has been involved with efforts to recover and identify the remains of American military personnel lost in action. The CILHI has identified more than 1,100 individuals from World War II, the Korean War and the Vietnam War.

Heretofore, CILHI has based its identifications primarily on the analysis of recovered bones and teeth. More recently, it has turned to the emerging science of mitochondrial DNA (mtDNA) for use in more difficult cases. For example, in 1998, CILHI successfully relied on mtDNA technology to identify the Vietnam remains in the Tomb of the Unknown Soldier in Arlington National Cemetery. More than 400 American service members have been identified through mtDNA technology.

To resolve doubts about Lell's identification, in 1999 Willey submitted a tooth from CNC Grave 453 to the CILHI for DNA analysis. A year later, the tooth was transferred to the Armed Forces DNA Identification Laboratory, Rockville, Md., where mtDNA was extracted, amplified and sequenced. A total of 425 base pairs (out of a typical 611) were sequenced from the tooth.

Two maternal relatives of Lell provided a few drops of blood for comparison to the results obtained from the tooth. Six hundred ten bases were generated from each of the two maternal relatives. When a comparison was made, the sequence from the maternal references was different from the sequence from the CNC Grave 453 tooth. Both sequences were unique when compared to a mtDNA database of 4,142 unrelated individuals, suggesting relatively rare mtDNA types. Willey concluded, "The skeleton previously believed to be Lell's could not be from a maternal relative of these blood donors." While this individual has proved not to be Lell, Willey remains optimistic that testing will eventually identify Lell as the occupant of grave 454, 456 or 458 in Custer National Cemetery.

---

[1] Information about the DNA testing in connection with this set of remains was provided by P. Willey. Full results of his testing will be published in the May 2004 issue of *Greasy Grass* magazine.

FARRIER VINCENT CHARLEY

The unfortunate tale of Farrier Vincent Charley is one of the best-known sidebar stories in Little Bighorn lore. As Company D retreated from Weir Point, a bullet wound to his hips prevented Charley from making his own way back to the defense perimeter. Lt. W. S. Edgerley claimed he was forbidden to rescue the wounded trooper, who was urged, somewhat strangely, to hide himself in a nearby ravine until he could be rescued later. Before his comrades could return, the luckless Charley was killed by the Indians. The exact site is unknown, but is generally thought to be in the vicinity of Cedar Coulee, although a modern marble marker sits just off the battlefield road 2,000 feet south of Weir Point. Scott checked that area with a metal detector in 1994, but failed to find any remains or artifacts to support that location.

Charley first enlisted on March 4, 1871, at Chicago. According to his enlistment record, he was born in Lucerne, Switzerland, and had worked as a farmer. He was 22 years old, stood 5 feet 10 1/4 inches tall, and had hazel eyes, red hair and a sandy complexion. He reenlisted March 5, 1876, at Fort Abraham Lincoln, Dakota Territory, where Capt. Thomas B. Weir appointed him as Company D's farrier.

According to the analysis of Burial 4, exhumed from National Cemetery Grave 455, the individual was a fairly robust white male in the 25-30-year range and 5 feet 10.7 inches tall. His dental health had been poor, as he was missing a number of teeth and others showed signs of disease. The skeleton displayed several previous injuries, including broken bones that had healed. As was true of many troopers, he showed indications of disk problems in his back, which would have caused severe pain. Another more recent injury, however, was more important in identifying this individual. That injury, a gunshot wound to the right hip bone, or ileum, that showed no signs of healing, likely occurred at the time of his death. The bullet entered the bone from the person's right and back and produced a perforation above the hip joint. Metal fragments that the bullet left adjacent to the hole and in the nearby tailbone, or sacrum, confirmed a gunshot wound as the cause of injury. No indications of bullet impact were found on the bones of the person's left side. The bullet, after passing through the man's right hip, likely passed through organs of the abdomen and exited from the left abdominal wall.

Scott narrowed the man's identity to five possibilities, but Charley seemed the most likely candidate, thanks to the hip wound he was known to have suffered. Also, the study indicated the man was age 25-30; Charley was 27 in 1876. Their heights were almost an exact match — Charley at 5 feet 10 1/4 inches and the skeleton at just shy of 5 feet 10 3/4 inches. Scott noted the skeletal remains appeared silent about confirming one aspect of Charley's death — the reported jamming of a stick down his throat. Scott said, "The skeleton is frustratingly ambiguous on whether a stick was jammed down its throat." The individual's skull also gave no evidence of a head wound some accounts say Charley had sustained, but Scott speculated that such a wound might have merely damaged flesh, not bone, if it occurred at all. In the end, Scott concluded, "It is highly likely that the skeleton in Grave 455 is Charley."

OTHER BATTLE-RELATED REMAINS

In either 1925 or 1926, another set of human remains was recovered during excavation for a culvert. C.H. Asbury, the superintendent for Crow Agency, reported a human skeleton, nearly complete except for the skull, was found about 500 or 600 feet from the marker in the Little Bighorn Valley for Lt. Donald I. McIntosh in line with a marker for scout Charley Reynolds. Both men were killed during Reno's retreat. However, rancher Henry Weibert claimed the remains were found by his father and him in 1925, about one quarter mile east of the Garryowen store, while they were putting in a culvert. The body was reburied in a special cenotaph during the 50th battle anniversary celebration in 1926. No matter which story is correct, this set of remains has never undergone forensic examination. Today, it rests in its grave in front of the Garryowen Trading Post.

In 1928, two burials occurred in Grave 942. Custer Battlefield Supt. Eugene Wessenger wrote in an Oct. 26, 1928, letter to the Quartermaster General that two days earlier he had found a skeleton buried about one foot deep on unplowed land 300 feet from the Reno Retreat crossing. After the skeleton was exhumed, it was buried in the cemetery Oct. 25 in the same grave where another body had been buried Aug. 1. The August remains supposedly were found 300 yards south of the battlefield's boundary fence. According to accounts, the skeleton had an arrow sticking in its backbone. A leather artifact found near the body bore the initials J.D. or R.D. Analysis of these two sets of remains provided the experts with a surprise. Part of the remains from the Reno retreat area were not those of a soldier, but instead of an older Native American female, who likely had died from a severe disease. In 1994, rancher Jason Pitsch, who owns the land, found additional remains. A team from the Midwest Archeological Center examined the site more closely and removed additional bone material that tests confirmed were likely related to the earlier discovered female as well as a second soldier. Eventually, the remains of the Native American woman were returned to her people for proper burial in accordance with the Native American Graves Protection and Repatriation Act of 1990. Scott sees this occurrence as a reminder that the Little Bighorn Battle site has been used by a varied number of people across the centuries and that not everything found in the valley relates to the events of 1876.

Two other unknowns from the Custer Battlefield area were buried in Grave 517A sometime before 1940, according to battlefield correspondence. But the records provided Scott with no additional information about the time or place where the bodies were recovered.

In summing up their analysis of the various remains from the national cemetery, Scott and P. Willey determined that these men "lived rugged, active lives." At least five had fractures that had healed prior to death. At least three showed degenerative disease affecting joints, especially in the spine. They concluded: "These changes are most frequent and most severe in the mid-to-lower back and are especially surprising considering the relatively young age of most of the soldiers. It is likely that their long days in the saddle caused — or at least was a major contributing factor to — these changes. Translated into more humanistic terms, many of the cavalrymen suffered from severe, nearly disabling back pain."

They noted, too, the oral health of the men was poor by modern standards. Each soldier had lost at least an average of three teeth, if not more, and all showed signs of other severe dental disease. Many exhibited stains suggesting they had used tobacco in some form.

Analysis also revealed details about how the men died and what may have happened to their bodies after their deaths. Six of the men had been shot, three in the skull. One man, likely Charley, had been wounded in the hip with the bullet passing through the abdomen. X-rays disclosed metal fragments in the proximal humerus of the fifth man, suggesting he sustained an arm wound. The sixth individual had metal particles in a few bones of the abdomen, suggesting he had been wounded there.

Many of the remains showed signs of cuts inflicted after death. At least two had marks on the skulls suggesting they may have been scalped. Others exhibited cuts near extremities, suggesting attempts at dismemberment. The individual designated as Burial 7 may have endured genital removal as well as no fewer than 98 other cuts. Not surprisingly, the bodies known to have been killed on Reno-Benteen displayed fewer cuts than those killed on Custer battlefield.

EARLIER RECOVERY OF REMAINS AT THE BATTLEFIELD

In the 1991 *Greasy Grass*, Scott and co-author Douglas Owsley wrote about several of the earliest documented recovery of human remains from the battlefield. According to one of their stories, in April 1886, Hospital Steward James Carroll of Fort Custer discovered an incomplete skull, which he donated to the Army Medical Museum in 1889 as

Sharon Long of ID Images completed this facial reconstruction from the Shufeldt skull, but the individual has never been identified.
(Victor Krantz)

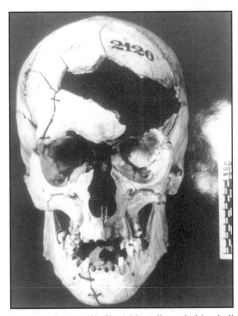

Surgeon Robert W. Shufeldt collected this skull from the battlefield in 1877 for study at the Army Medical Museum, Washington, D.C.
(Victor Krantz)

specimen 1001064. Carroll apparently found the skull cap in a ravine about 1,000 yards from the Monument — probably Deep Ravine. According to the article, "The skull cap exhibited significant trauma including a large-caliber gunshot entry wound in the back of the head, with an exit wound in the middle of the forehead over the left eye. The size of the exit wound, 26mm in diameter, is much larger than the entrance opening in the occipital bone (18mm)."

In addition, cut marks on the top of the skull suggested the individual had been scalped. Embedded in the bone was the tip of an iron arrowhead or knife. Their analysis indicated the remains probably belonged to a white male, age 27-35. Unfortunately, more than 80 men who died with Custer fit this age range, so no identification of the individual has been possible.

The two experts also reported on an earlier discovery by Assistant Surgeon Robert W. Shufeldt, who visited Custer battlefield with a scouting party of Company I, 5th U.S. Cavalry, in July 1877 and collected a human skull, not as a souvenir, but as a medical specimen. The skull and mandible Shufeldt collected were sent to the Army Medical Museum in Washington, D.C., in July 1881. Reportedly a Sioux Indian with the 5th Cavalry who had seen the soldier killed pointed out the remains to the doctor. The authors stated, "According to Shufeldt's correspondence with the Army Medical Museum, the Indian reported the man was among the first killed in the charge on the Indian camp. After he was killed, the Sioux stated, the man's face was mutilated by a war club wielded by an Indian woman. Shufeldt presumed the man to be a bugler because of the double yellow stripes found on his rotting trousers, and further assumed him to be a trumpeter of Company M killed in Reno's charge on the Cheyenne camp. The basis for these assumptions is not indicated."

How accurate Shufeldt was is unclear today. For one, only officers, sergeants and corporals were authorized to wear a trouser stripe, each of a specific width. Musicians weren't authorized to wear double yellow trouser stripes until 1883. Apparently some commanding officers, including Custer, may have allowed band members to wear such stripes earlier than that. Lt. Charles DeRudio testified during the Reno Court of Inquiry in 1879 that one trumpeter was identified "from the marks on the pants."

Today, the skull and the two uppermost vertebrae are in the Smithsonian Institution. Examination of these remains revealed the individual was a white male, between age 27 and 35, with gracile features. He apparently had suffered from dental problems, as three teeth were lost earlier in life and cavities were present in five molars. The skull exhibits blunt instrument trauma to the left frontal and temporal areas, and some evidence suggests a heavy sharp instrument landed a blow to the left cheek area. In seeking to identify the man, Scott eliminated trumpeters from Company M, as none of them was killed. However, 11 trumpeters from other companies were killed, but of those with Custer, five are either too old or too young to be a candidate, or their bodies were identified elsewhere. That left trumpeters Thomas Bucknell, Henry Dose, William Kramer, Thomas McElroy and Thomas Way as possible candidates.

Of these candidates, only Henry Dose's body was identified by his comrades. According to accounts, Dose was found halfway between the Custer and Reno fields with arrows in his back and sides; between Deep Coulee and Medicine Tail Coulee; or near the ford at Medicine Tail Coulee. Scott and Owsley decided that could be broadly interpreted as the area where Shufeldt found the skull. The two experts considered other men of the Custer battalion as possibilities. They eliminated the three officers who were not definitely identified — Lt. James Porter, Lt. James G. Sturgis and Lt. Henry M. Harrington — as too young. That left 19 sergeants and nine corporals within the age criteria.

This skull found by Shufeldt was sent to Sharon Long of ID Images, another specialist in facial reconstruction of forensic cases. They compared the likeness she prepared to known photographs of the men, but no matches were noted. Of the 19 sergeant candidates, nine had known photographs. That left 10 (James Bustard, William Cashan, Martin Considine, August Finckle, William James, Michael Kenney, Frederick Nursey, William Sharrow, Amos Warren and DeWitt Winney) as possibilities. Of the nine corporals, three were photographed, leaving six candidates (Otto Hagemann, William Harrison, James Martin, Henry Mason, George Morris and William Teeman). Of the trumpeters, only Thomas Way was photographed, leaving the others as potential candidates. Historical information indicated Considine, Finckle, Hagemann, Martin, Sharrow, Winney and Teeman were identified elsewhere on the battlefield, probably eliminating them from further consideration. That left the other 13 soldiers as candidates for the identity whose face may appear in the reconstruction.

So what does all of this mean? Scott's concluding paragraph to his 1991 *Greasy Grass* article spoke to that point: "The osteobiography of the men who died with Custer is developing slowly. The bones described here add to that file, a tangible link to the men themselves. Bones, even if they are not identifiable to an individual, tell how men died, and much about their health, diet and way of life. These details are not often recorded by history and yet they are a reminder that we are dealing with the physical remains of flesh and blood characters, whose lives were cut short as a result of cultures in conflict. Though such details may seem unimportant in relation to the epic event of the battle, as the number grows through ongoing research, and are brought together, patterns could emerge that will increase understanding of the course of the battle and the lives of the men who fought it."

Material for this chapter was derived from interviews with Doug Scott as well as the following articles and reports:

• Connor, Melissa, *Exhumation of Human Remains on the Pitsch Property near Little Bighorn National Battlefield, Montana* (Lincoln, Neb.: National Park Service Midwest Archeological Center, 1994)
   • Glenner, Richard A., Willey, P., and Scott, Douglas D., "Back to the Little Bighorn," *Journal of the American Dental Association*, July 1994, pp. 835-843
   • Glenner, Richard A., Willey, P., and Scott, Douglas D., "Oral Health of Seventh Cavalry Troopers: Dentitions from the Custer National Cemetery," *Journal of the History of Dentristy*, March 1996, pp. 3-14
   • Scott, Douglas D. and Owsley, Douglas, "Oh, what tales bones could tell — and often do!", *Greasy Grass*, May 1991, pp. 33-39
   • Scott, Douglas D. and Willey, P., "Custer's men took names to their graves," *Greasy Grass*, May 1996, pp. 20-28
   • Scott, Douglas D. and Willey, P., "The Custer Battlefield National Cemetery Human Remains Identification Project," *8th annual Symposium Book*, Custer Battlefield Historical & Museum Association, June 24, 1994, Hardin, Mont.
   • Scott, Douglas D. and Willey, P., "'The Bullets Buzzed Like Bees;' Gunshot Wounds in Skeletons from the Battle of the Little Bighorn," *International Journal of Osteoarchaeology*, 1996, pp. 15-27
   • Thackeray, Lorna, "Experts trace facial bones to Custer interpreter Boyer," *Billings Mont. Gazette*, Oct. 26, 1986, p. 1A
   • Willey, P., *Human Osteology of the Pitsch Burials*, (Lincoln, Neb.: National Park Service Midwest Archeological Center, 1994)

Chapter Nine

CUSTER'S REBURIAL

AT WEST POINT

Custer's grave as it appears today at West Point

(Sandy Barnard)

Digging Into Custer's Last Stand

Some years ago, my research into the life of First Sgt. John Ryan took me to the Massachusetts Military Archives, then located in Natick, a suburban town west of Boston. En route I passed through another town, Wellesley. Later, a television news report recounted a tragedy along the same road I had traveled. A parked car, its engine running, had slipped into gear, surged across the street and plowed through a group of investment bankers. One woman, on a business trip to Wellesley from New Jersey, had been killed instantly and several companions badly injured.

The TV news story quoted one of the dead woman's stunned companions: "We were just going to lunch. That's something you do every day. Until one day you head for lunch and, instead, you end up dead."

I was struck by the parallel between what the victim's friend had said and what I imagined Ryan and fellow survivors of the Battle of Little Bighorn must have felt as they gazed upon the scene before them on the Custer field. They must have had great difficulty reconciling the sight of the dead Custer and their dead comrades with images of the victims enjoying boundless energy in life just days earlier.

On June 27, 1876, Lt. James Bradley and his scouts came upon the bodies of Custer and his men, two days after their deaths. Bradley, perhaps the first white man to gaze on the carnage along the Little Bighorn, called it an "appalling sight...his entire command in the embrace of death."

Bradley described Custer's wounds as "scarcely discoverable" and he appeared to have died "a natural death." To Bradley, Custer's "expression was rather that of a man who had fallen asleep and enjoyed peaceful dreams than that of one who had met his death amid such fearful scenes as that field had witnessed, the features being wholly without ghastliness or an impress of fear, horror, or despair. He had died as he had lived — a hero — and excited the remark of those who had known him and saw him there, 'You could almost imagine him standing before you!' Such was Custer at the time of his burial, on the 28th of June, three days after the fight in which he had fallen...."

Placing the coffin on the caisson at the dock. **(Sandy Barnard)**

After laying in the hot Montana sun for three days, Custer's body would have been more ghastly than Bradley and others were willing to express in that Victorian era. Still, Custer and the other dead on that field had to be buried during the next two days by their surviving comrades.

Not surprisingly, the task of identifying the dead was nearly impossible. Their wounds and postmortem mutilation by the Indians, along with the bloating and decomposition resulting from several days in the hot sun, made their identification that much more difficult. So, each of the dead was buried close to where he had fallen, the historical record suggests, but a lack of proper tools meant that most men were thinly

The remains of General Custer in the vault at Poughkeepsie
(Sandy Barnard)

covered at best. Few of the crude stakes erected over the hastily dug graves bore names of the 7th Cavalry dead.

An exception was made for Custer himself. Ryan claimed he led an enlisted detail from Company M that buried many of the men who had fallen around Custer on Last Stand Hill, including Capt. Thomas W. Custer and Lt. W. W. Cooke, Custer's adjutant. His lengthy account details the condition of the bodies and the burials:

"Gen. Custer was not scalped. He had two bullet wounds — one through his head from one side to the other, another through his body. We found those bodies on a little gravelly knoll surrounded by quite a few bodies of other men.

"We dug a grave about 18 inches deep and put the General in. We then found another body. We could not tell who it was because it was terribly mutilated. Some thought it was Capt. Custer and others differed.

"There has been quite a controversy between different parties in regard to the body of Capt. Custer. Some claimed that his body was mutilated and others said it was not. Capt. Custer's head was crushed in as flat as a man's hand. He was slit

Site of the proposed place of burial at West Point
(Sandy Barnard)

Bearing the remains to the cemetery   **(Sandy Barnard)**

down through the center of his body and also through the muscles of both arms, also slit down through both thighs and disfigured in other ways....

"I knew that Capt. Custer had T.W.C. marked on his arm with India ink because I was more or less familiar with him in camp, as he was first lieutenant of my troop for four years before he was made captain of C Troop. We examined the body thoroughly and we found the letters T.W.C. and that settled it.

"We then laid him beside the General in the same grave and covered them over with pieces of tents and blankets and mounded the grave over with dirt. We found an Indian travois and turned it upside down over the grave and we spiked it down with wooded pins, and we laid stones around it to keep the wolves from digging them up. That was the best burial that I saw of any of the bodies on the field."

Ryan's description of the burial of the Custers as the "best" on the field is important. Their more complete burial should have ensured their easy recovery later. But that proved untrue in June 1877, when an armed expedition, commanded by Capt. Michael V. Sheridan, returned to the battlefield to recover the bodies of Custer and the other officers. The scene they found made it obvious their task would not be easy. Despite the apparent care of Ryan's detail the year before, the military reburial party encountered problems determining which body was Custer's. Sheridan's men found wind and rain had eroded many of the graves and the markers had been scattered. Too, the remains were more or less completely skeletonized. The soldiers eventually exhumed 10 skeletons, including one they believed to be Custer's. The bodies of Custer's youngest brother, Boston, and his nephew, Autie Reed, were recovered and sent to Michigan for burial. Still, considerable doubt exists today as to whether Custer's body was properly identified by Sheridan's party, and whether it was truly the general's remains that were buried at West Point, N.Y., later that year.

In their 1989 book, *Archaeological Perspectives on the Battle of the Little Big Horn,* Scott and Fox say:

"Whether the exhumed skeletons were actually those of the officers and civilians under whose names they were buried also seems questionable. As already mentioned, because of the condition of the corpses, it is possible that some were incorrectly identified after the battle. To this uncertainty must be added the difficulties the exhumation team apparently encountered in locating the graves.

"Some hint of the problem is provided by the fact that, after removing the skeleton from the grave first thought to be Custer's, it was discovered that a rotting uniform blouse found with the bones contained the name of a 7th Cavalry corporal. Baffled, the searchers then opened a second grave near the first. It was found to contain only a skull, rib cage and femur. For one reason or another — possibly because there was no evidence to the contrary— the searchers were satisfied these bones were those of Custer."

The soldiers on the recovery team may have had doubts about this identification. One reportedly said, "It was a disconcerting discovery to find that even the general could not be satisfactorily identified."

Again, based on Ryan's description of the Custer brothers' burial, their recovery should not have caused so many problems. The archeologists suggested, "While far

141

Bearing Custer's remains to
the cemetery
(Sandy Barnard)

The service in the chapel
(Sandy Barnard)

from Pharaonic, such an internment should have been sufficient to protect the bodies from the elements and animal scavengers, which combined to expose the shallower graves of the lesser dead. One would expect, therefore, that the exhumation team would have found two complete sets of remains instead of a single partial skeleton. It also seems strange that they apparently found no remnants of the blankets and canvas sheets used to cover the bodies."

But with Custer a national hero and his legend already blossoming, Sheridan needed to return with a body, and so he did. The right body? Probably not.

The archeologists point out that if the well-marked grave holding the Custers could not be properly located, no doubt at least some of the other officers and civilians were not properly recovered either. They concluded:

"There exists the possibility, at least, that one or more unknown troopers may be perpetually doomed to the commission of that most cardinal of military sins: impersonating an officer. If so, it also follows that the bones of one or more of the officers or of Custer's civilian kinsmen may now either lie commingled with those of the enlisted men in the common grave under the granite monument or in a solitary grave overlooked by the reburial party when they transferred the skeletons to the common grave in 1881."

Other experts also have voiced their doubts about the Custer burial to the news media. For example, forensic anthropologist Clyde Snow told the *Los Angeles Times* in 1991, "I have a suspicion they got the wrong body." Snow, who has studied the records of the Custer burial and exhumation, added, "It would be ironic if some buck private were buried up there at West Point."

The article quoted Doug McChristian, then chief historian at Little Bighorn Battlefield National Monument: "I've often thought in my own warped way that Libbie was sure surprised if there was some corporal lying beside her." On her death in 1933, Libbie was buried beside her husband at West Point.

"The thought that it might not be Custer is too delicious to put to rest," Snow said. If someone other than Custer was buried there, "they'd probably put the poor guy out somewhere."

Snow further suggested that "The only way to put those suspicions to bed would be to look at the bones interred at West Point and see how they gibe with information we have on General Custer." Snow said that, from a professional standpoint, he would like to dig Custer up and try to identify the remains. But as someone who enjoys myths, he prefers the idea of maintaining the mystery about the occupant of Custer's West Point grave.

In the *L.A. Times* article Scott also pointed out that the haphazard recovery of Custer's body by Sheridan's men should not be considered surprising, as such carelessness was typical of the times. A century ago, a tomb or monument to honor the dead was more important than preserving the actual remains.

"In the cultural context of the day, the attitude about dying was to memorialize the death rather than worry about the corpus itself," he said. "Their attitude was to go for a skull, maybe some ribs, an arm or a leg, and that was enough."

At least one contemporary newspaper, *Frank Leslie's Illustrated*, took note of the controversy on Oct. 20, 1877: "Although the remains of General Custer, and

Carrying the remains to the grave

(Sandy Barnard)

The last honors over the grave

(Sandy Barnard)

most of his friends…had evidently been disfigured by the coyotes or savages, and probably both, and many, if not the most, of the skulls there and throughout all the fields were smashed to fragments, mangled or missing, still what was decided to be and probably were the main portions of the bones of General Custer and his two brothers were secured…The remains were carefully gathered, wrapped and then packed with grass cut from Custer's Valley…."

The newspaper observed, "All that was left of General Custer was forwarded East without delay…."

Right or wrong, Captain Sheridan had a body that he reported as Custer's. On his return to Fort Abraham Lincoln, he telegraphed Mrs. Custer for further instructions about burying the general. Wanting her husband buried at West Point, Mrs. Custer conferred with Maj. Gen. John H. Schofield, the military academy's commandant. She wrote Sheridan that she had arranged for the burial service to be delayed until October or November "as there will then be a full corps of cadets and officers at West point and he [Schofield] can be better able to pay the honor he wishes to the heroic dead." In the interim, the "sacred dust" was placed in a receiving vault in early August at Poughkeepsie under the care of Philip Hamilton.

The funeral — full of military pomp — was held Wednesday, Oct. 10, 1877. The *New York Herald* reported "A large concourse of people" attended the service. The *New York Times* said that "From every city, town and hamlet on the Hudson people came to participate in the last, sad rites due so brave a soldier."

The *Times* added, "The morning had been gloomy, a dense fog enveloping everything…soon the sun broke through the clouds, the fog lifted, and a cool northerly breeze swept through the valleys."

According to the newspapers, the funeral procession at Poughkeepsie formed at 9 a.m. and included a platoon of police, the 21st Regiment Band, Brig. Gen. George Parker and staff of the 8th Brigade, a battalion of the 21st Infantry, cadets of the Poughkeepsie Military Institute, Bald Eagle Battery, and clergy. The hearse, drawn by four coal-black horses, was decorated with flags and black crape. The metallic casket was draped with a flag, reportedly the one of Capt. Louis Hamilton, who had been killed during Custer's battle at the Washita in November 1868. A single floral arrangement adorned the head of the casket, forming a major general's shoulder strap, two feet long by eight inches wide, the background woven of geraniums and the stars of tube roses. Custer had risen to the rank of major general during the Civil War.

By 10:30 a.m., the remains were placed in the ladies saloon aboard the steamer *Mary Powell*. As the steamer approached the south dock at West Point, two other steamers, the *Hopkins* and *Henry Smith*, appeared, bearing other civilian and military dignitaries. A detachment of cavalry escorted the casket to the chapel for the services which began at 2:15 p.m. Custer's helmet and saber were placed on the casket. At the foot was a beautiful wreath encircling the words, "Seventh Cavalry."

The service was brief. The Rev. John Forsythe, West Point's chaplain, read part of the Episcopal burial service and a choir of cadets chanted the 39th and 90th Psalms. Among those present, according to the newspapers, were Custer's widow, Libbie, attended by Schofield; Custer's father Emanuel; Mary Barrett, the wife of his close friend, the actor Lawrence Barrett; and other family and friends. Outside the chapel the West Point cadets lined up on one side of the roadway, while other military organizations formed on the opposite side.

"Mrs. Custer, leaning upon the arm of General Schofield, followed the remains closely, and was deeply affected, shedding tears freely, as did General Custer's father and sister," The *Times* reported.

A lengthy military procession escorted the remains to the cemetery on the north post overlooking the Hudson River. The band played the funeral march. At the grave the balance of the burial service was read. "Here the body was lowered into its last resting place, earth was sprinkled upon it," The Times stated. Three volleys were fired in salute by the corps of cadets.

Harper's Weekly reported, "The echoes reverberated from side to side of the river, flung back from cliff to cliff, and died mournfully away. The funeral services were over, and the body of the brave Custer was left to rest where his comrades had laid him."

By 4 p.m., the ceremonies were complete.

A separate controversy surrounds the statue of Custer that was placed at West Point in 1879. Hated from the beginning by Mrs. Custer, the monument was removed in late 1884 at her insistence and stored in a shed. By 1905, the pedestal had been moved to the Custer grave and mounted with a Washington Monument-like shaft that remains today. What happened to the statue remains a mystery. The head and shoulders apparently were cut off in 1906, but the resulting bust has never been seen since.

Much about George Custer created controversy in his lifetime. We should not be surprised that aspects of his burial and reburial have also resulted in lingering controversy. During analysis of the remains removed from the National Cemetery in 1992, Doug Scott added a new wrinkle to this story. Burial 8B, one of the pre-1940 burials that lacked further details, contained an incomplete skeleton that lacked its skull and most of the postcranial remains. He determined the individual was between 35 and 40 years of age and stood 71.3 inches tall. Of all the Little Bighorn casualties, guess who best matched such a profile? None other than Custer himself, age 36 at his death. He also was 71 inches tall.

Of further interest, Scott pointed out that onlookers noted that Custer's body bore bullet wounds in his left temple and in his chest, either in the upper chest or lower. Lab study of Burial 8B showed the skeleton had metal fragments in bones adjacent to the abdomen, indicating a gunshot wound.

Before anyone should jump to the conclusion that at least a portion of the remains of Custer rests in the Custer Battlefield National Cemetery, several findings suggest another possibility. For example, Burial 8B's teeth showed a groove suggesting he was a pipe smoker. Custer probably did not smoke. This individual had other problems as well. The experts found signs of degenerative joint disease in the spine, indicating the man had a bad back. He may have had a temporomandibular joint problem, which would have made chewing a problem. Thirdly, two ribs had signs of long healed breaks. Custer was not known to have had any of these problems. Finally, Burial 8B's oral heath was terrible.

146

Scott concluded, "Such poor dental care and health would be surprising for someone of Custer's social standing."

Was Burial 8B George Custer? In the end, Scott decided, "This identification is so tenuous, however, that rather than claiming that Burial 8B is Custer, it is more accurate to say that Custer cannot be excluded as a possibility."

That should mean that Libbie Custer can continue to rest with some assurance that the soldier beside her is indeed her husband.

Chapter Ten

DIGGING IN THE VALLEY

First-time visitors to Little Bighorn Battlefield National Monument are immediately struck by its apparent pristine condition, unlike many Civil War battlefields in the East, which are threatened by modern encroachment. But throughout the more than 127 years since the Little Bighorn battle, that field, too, has been impacted by man. In 1881, before the three sections of granite could be erected on Last Stand Hill as a lasting memorial to the 7th U.S. Cavalry, the knoll itself was graded. To what degree that occurred remains unclear. Later, the public access road was installed around the edge of the knoll and a parking lot constructed beside it, forever altering the true appearance of the site where George Custer died. In 2003, the new Indian Memorial was dedicated on a knoll across the road from the 7th Cavalry Monument.

By 1879, Custer battlefield had been designated a fourth class cemetery by the U.S government. Today's national cemetery stretches across a ridge that likely saw significant combat in 1876. Likewise, the Reno-Benteen Defense Site, four miles to the south of the main battlefield, has endured construction of the access road and a parking lot in the heart of the 7th Cavalry's defensive perimeter. En route to that location, the road cuts through another important battlefield landmark at Weir Point.

In the Little Bighorn Valley itself is the important site where Major Marcus A. Reno ordered his charging battalion to halt to establish a skirmish line against the warriors pouring out of the village to meet the 7th Cavalry's challenge, but it, too, has been significantly undermined by modern development. The valley has been a farming and ranching mecca since the first settlers entered the region shortly after

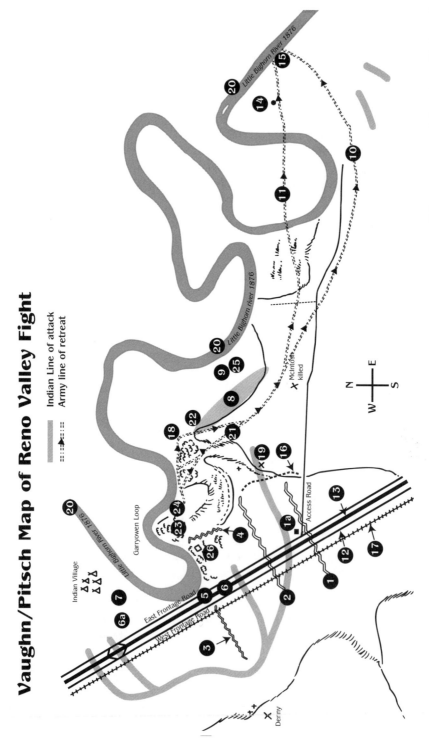

Vaughn/Pitsch Map of Reno Valley Fight

Indian Line of attack
Army line of retreat

(Map prepared by Gary Raham)

150

MAP LEGEND

1. Reno's initial skirmish line (Pitsch)
1a. Reno Battlefield Museum site 1997
2. Reno's initial skirmish line, advanced position (Pitsch)
3. Reno's initial skirmish line (Vaughn)
4. Reno's timber fight line (Vaughn)
5. Original Garryowen store site
6. Original 1926 unknown soldier monument
6a. Relocated unknown soldier monument
7. Modern Garryowen Trading Post / Conoco service station (and site of 1960s Garryowen store and post office)
8. Reno's timber fight line (Pitsch)
9. Park site within timber (Pitsch)
10. Reno's main retreat route (Vaughn)
11. Alternate retreat route taken by some of Reno's men
12. Original Highway 87 (West Frontage Road)
13. Interstate Highway 90 / Highway 87

14. Unknown soldier grave marker
15. Reno's retreat crossing
16. Fall back of Reno's skirmish line (Pitsch)
17. Burlington Northern Railroad tracks
18. Reno's exit from timber (Vaughn)
19. Charley Reynolds' death site (Vaughn)
20. Approximate course of Little Bighorn River in 1876
21. Charley Reynolds' death site (Pitsch)
22. Reynolds and other scouts on right of timber line (Pitsch)
23. Reynolds and other scouts on right of timber line (Vaughn)
24. Led horses (Vaughn)
25. Led horses (Pitsch)
26. Caplett House

Digging Into Custer's Last Stand

Jason Pitsch's research suggests Reno's first skirmish line took shape in the field in front of the Reno Battlefield Museum building.   **(Sandy Barnard)**

the battle. Across the decades irrigation projects have altered the course of the river itself and other streams in the area. In the mid-1890s, the Chicago, Burlington and Quincy Railroad line — today the Burlington Northern line — bisected the valley, but nothing more assaulted the historical integrity of the opening arena of the Reno fight than construction of Interstate Highway 90 , especially its interchange at Garryowen. To provide for the interchange, tons of dirt were moved or added to create the approach for a bridge — essentially in the middle of the skirmish line position and ruining the view shed of the historic site.

Despite all these man-made insults to the historic nature of the ground, surprisingly the Little Bighorn still yields clues to the battle, including Reno's engagement. Rancher Jason Pitsch's family owned land associated with the valley fight for several generations. His great-grandfather, along with three brothers, arrived in the valley at the turn of the century to raise sugar beets. Over the years the family's holdings grew to some 10,000 acres, although farming and ranching, not historical preservation, motivated their efforts.

Pitsch said, "It [Expansion] didn't have anything to do with the battle."

But in 1989, in the wake of his fascination with the archeological projects, his own interests began to change. For many years, as he worked his fields, an occasional battle-related artifact would surface. After reading archeological accounts of their work by Scott and Fox, Pitsch began inventorying his own property. "I kinda got an idea of how they did it," he explains, "but since I didn't have the sophisticated

Jason Pitsch's discovery of artifacts along the tree line and the high area on the right has convinced him that this now-open field was the site of Reno's timber fight in 1876. **(Sandy Barnard)**

equipment they had used, I started marking each cartridge with a number, cataloging it and marking it on a topographical map that I blew on up and then detailed it, putting in the different items. I kind of learned things myself by reading."

During his research, he discovered some 9,000 artifacts associated with soldier, Indian and settler life in the Little Bighorn Valley. His battle-related material was displayed for a time in the now-defunct Reno Battlefield Museum on a corner of his property at Garryowen. Although the historical integrity of the site of his building was forever altered by the I-90 highway construction, his metal detecting in the field in front of the structure revealed a soldier position he believes was the original skirmish line for Reno's troops facing their onrushing foe on the afternoon of June 25. More important, he developed a significant new theory about the subsequent course of the Reno action, including pinpointing an area on his property that he believes marks the actual site of the timber fight.

Locations of the various sites associated with Reno's opening segment of the battle have been debated for years. Theories of three earlier researchers about where actions along the skirmish line and in the timber took place have been generally considered important. In the 1930s, Fred Dustin believed the Garryowen Loop had been dry in 1876, only to be naturally refilled with water between 1876 and 1891. In 1923, this loop was cut off intentionally by the railroad. Dustin theorized the timber fight site was part of the then-dry Garryowen Loop. However, researchers today place little faith in this as early maps, including those of Philetus Norris in

1877, Oscar Long in 1878 and John T. Blake in 1883, clearly show an active Garryowen Loop.

In 1951, researcher Charles Kuhlman advanced his theory that placed the timber one loop back — upstream or southeast of the Garry-owen Loop. Finally, in 1966, J.W. Vaughn used a metal detector to search the countryside and to align artifactual evidence with that of history and geography. He believed Reno's first skirmish line was aligned east to west, with the east end of the line resting on what became the site of the Old Garryowen store. However, he positioned the timber fight itself behind the Old Garryowen store and the Albert Caplett house in what today is essentially an area of steep banked river bed and swampland. With that view, he was closer to Dustin than to Kuhlman in his thinking.

According to Vaughn's interpretation, Reno then retreated from the timber through the open field north of the access road to the Pitsch property. In that field are markers to three individuals killed on the retreat: scout Charley Reynolds, interpreter Isaiah Dorman and Lt. Donald McIntosh. Since that time, Vaughn's views have held sway about the presumed location of the timber fight of Reno's troops.

Among the three, Kuhlman's timber theory may have been given less credence by students of the battle, but surprisingly, Pitsch, based on his own research through metal detecting on his property, believes Kuhlman may have been the most accurate. According to Pitsch's theory, Reno on his approach to the village reined in his troops and established a skirmish line that began essentially in his field where he has his museum today. It likely stretched west across the modern road and rail bed. As warriors poured from the village, Reno moved his line forward perhaps 200 yards and angled this advanced skirmish line so it faced in two directions — toward the Indians, advancing from the low hills in the west, who were attempting to turn the left end of the skirmish line and toward the village itself. As pressure mounted on his troops, Reno had them shift position while maneuvering toward the timber, located much deeper on Pitsch's property.

Today the monument to Charley Reynolds stands just outside a spacious arena-like field that Pitsch believes is where Reno took refuge in the timber. In its openness, this area looks nothing like what one's imagination would suggest for a timber. However, Pitsch said the site was heavily brush-covered into the 1950s, when his grandfather and father cleared it for farming and ranch use. More important, in this field, particularly along its western edge, Pitsch uncovered large numbers of artifacts, including bullets and cartridge cases, during his metal detecting. A couple of hundred yards to the east the Little Bighorn River flows. The field itself is likely smaller than in 1876. A portion on the east collapsed later into the river during a flood.

Perhaps equally important, Pitsch has identified what may be two new sites of Indian villages. The first, north of the present-day Conoco gasoline station area — formerly the Garryowen Post Office — may well have been the location of the Hunkpapa camp circle. The second area is located on the east side of the river below Weir Point. Between May 10-14, 1993, Doug Scott led a project that mapped Pitsch's findings for future reference. In his report, Scott concluded about the second Indian encampment, "This location is unexpected and is an important new piece of information as no historic accounts clearly identify any Indian camps east of the river."

Scott noted, too, that Pitsch had found numerous fired cartridges, apparently Indian-related, on a bench just east of the second village site. He concluded, "The presence of those Indian associated cartridges cases as well as a few Army bullets suggest this may have been the site of a group of warriors who fired on the soldiers who were at Weir Point." He added that this new Indian combat position is "an important new contribution."

In the fields west of the old post office area, Pitsch found 11 .45-55 cartridge cases, which Scott interpreted as significant for they fell in a roughly linear alignment from northwest to southeast. He concluded, "Presumptively these cases identify Reno's first skirmish line. The angled alignment is more in keeping with an attack on the village site at Garry-owen than an east-west alignment as postulated by Vaughn [in 1966]."

Scott added, "A due east-west alignment would cause the soldiers to face obliquely away from the now identified camp sites." He suggests the Hunkpapa camp sat close to the river which flowed northwest. That would have meant the troops would have established their line at an angle to meet the warriors.

As further support for their belief that the northwest-southeast line represented Reno's skirmish line, Scott and Pitsch note the latter found some 25 .44 Henry, .50 Spencer and .50-70 cases during his metal detection on a bench to the west of the line, indicating an Indian firing position. "The location is consistent with the fact that Reno's line was outflanked and forced to fall back." They considered that farming may have disturbed the exact positions of these cartridges, but likely not the general linear alignment.

On a terrace above the Hunkpapa village site, Pitsch found seven .45-55 cases mixed in with seven .44 Henry cases, five .50-70 cases, a Spencer case and a round ball. Inasmuch as they seemed to lack a definite pattern, Scott concluded their disposition was consistent with the more irregular fighting patterns of the Indians.

In the area that Pitsch considers the site of the timber fight, Scott mapped only the perimeter itself, not individual artifact locations, because the soil, particularly along a slough, had been so disturbed by heavy

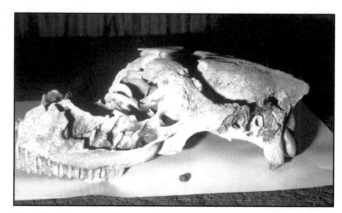

The .44 caliber bullet (foreground) was found by Jason Pitsch in the brain cavity of the horse skull. Artifacts with the animal's remains suggest it may have been ridden by Pvt. John Sivertsen, Company M.

(Sandy Barnard)

Digging Into Custer's Last Stand

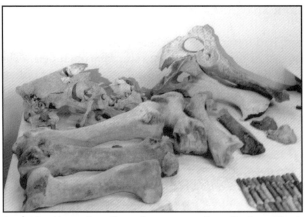

A considerable number of horse bones were collected by Jason Pitsch at a site on his ranch along the alternate retreat route used by fleeing men of Reno's battalion.

(Sandy Barnard)

equipment. However, his report offers an important conclusion: "If this is the timber fight area and if Vaughn and others are correct that the so-called Garryowen bend was active during the battle, then Reno's timber fight area was protected by the river on two sides. This may shed some light on comments by witnesses at the Reno Court of Inquiry that the timber area was defensible, suggesting a skirmish line could have been extended from river bank to river bank. The court witnesses and the archeological evidence suggest this did not occur, thus requiring the retreat to the ford."

Clusters of cases and bullets in other areas, including in the fields where the Reynolds, McIntosh and Dorman markers are located, also tend to support the historical record, Scott said. For example, Pitsch located "a significant cluster of Indian cases of all calibers...in the field adjacent to the [Custer Battlefield] Preservation Committee holdings that contain the retreat ford site. Again some Army cases were found in this general vicinity, but the large number of Indian cases, at least 30, indicate Reno's retreat was under pressure. These data very accurately confirm the historic accounts." The report notes, too, that a variety of miscellaneous items — from tin cans and percussion caps to horse tack and equipment — "are clearly intermingled with the Army cartridge cases and the Indian bullets."

In the village sites Pitsch discovered large quantities of Indian goods, but because of the effects of mny years of farming, Scott merely recorded areas of large concentrations rather than individual items. In the large village area in the summer of 1992, Pitsch found one of his more fascinating objects, a trade kettle with engraved images on it.

"I wasn't really looking for anything," he recalls. "I was working with irrigation when I spotted nearby a piece of metal which I recognized as historical brass. I gently turned it over and I noticed one of the horse's heads etched in it."

He showed it to Indian artifacts expert Putt Thompson and then-battlefield historian Doug McChristian. "They thought it was really amazing," Pitsch recalls.

Later, Scott took it to the lab for analysis. Speculation today is that the kettle art was drawn by Red Horse, whose ledger art drawings are at the Smithsonian.

"His ledger art drawings match the style of the drawings that are on the kettle," Pitsch explains. "Of course, the drawings on the kettle are a little more crude because it was probably drawn while sitting in camp."

ARTIFACTS FROM THE PITSCH DISCOVERIES

A collection of arrow points

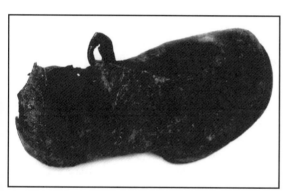

Cavalry boot apparently cut off by Indians.

**All photos by
Glen Swanson.**

Harmonica

Digging Into Custer's Last Stand

Another artifact important to him is a wedding ring that may have belonged to First Lt. Donald McIntosh, who had been buried where he fell on the Reno retreat route in 1876. A year later, his remains were exhumed and moved to the national cemetery at Fort Leavenworth, Kan. In 1909, McIntosh was reburied in Arlington National Cemetery. In the summer of 1995, Pitsch's metal detector alerted him to an object about 10 inches deep. Uncovering what appeared to be a ring, he cleaned it and noted the inscribed initials "D.M." and "M.M." as well as a partial date of "66." Glen Swanson, a collector of historical artifacts, suggested to Pitsch the ring belonged to McIntosh, who was given it by his wife Mollie at their wedding in 1866.

"Another really interesting find for me would be the horse skeleton, the bones and all the personal effects that were found around it," Pitsch says. He believes the animal and the objects with the skeleton belonged to 34-year-old Pvt. John Sivertsen, Company M, who enlisted in the 7th Cavalry in 1873. A native of Norway who had come to the United States in 1870, Sivertsen had been a blacksmith in civilian life. According to the historic record, he was among the men left behind in the timber when Reno launched his chaotic run for the river crossing. Unable to find his horse, Sivertsen stayed in the woods with Sgt. Charles White of Company M, five men of Company G and scout George Herendeen. Eventually, Sivertsen made his way to safety with the command on the bluffs.

Sivertsen later claimed he retrieved his horse from the river bottoms, unhurt with the soldier's blouse still hanging to the saddle. But Pitsch believes the horse was killed by a .44 caliber bullet he found in its brain cavity. Over a couple of years, Pitsch says, he uncovered not only the skeletal remains of a horse but a considerable amount of gear and ammunition in an area that generally corresponds to a secondary route used by the fleeing cavalrymen of Reno.

"Sivertsen actually couldn't find his horse in the timber line," Pitsch theorizes. "His horse probably took off following the rest of them [horses] for some reason and got shot down by Indians. Maybe it had been wounded previously."

He estimates he found about 60 percent of the animal's skeleton scattered with other artifacts in an almost perfect line of about 25 feet. According to his theory, the river's periodic floods scattered the objects. By using a metal detector, he located dozens of artifacts under several inches of dirt on the valley plain. His discoveries included various saddle parts; an 1874 mess kit; an 1872 spoon, knife and fork; an 1874 tin cup; a canteen; a curry comb; spectacles; a harmonica; and about 50 rounds of .45/55 caliber cartridges, .45 colt and .45 Schofield ammunition.

How did Glen Swanson and he tie the horse's remains and gear to Sivertsen? "It was in finding the bones that I came across the toothbrush," he says. "It had the initials J.S. on it, which is one of the ways we tied it to him."

However, four other men who fought in the valley also bore the initials J.S. Three of them — Pvt. John Seamans, Company M.; Pvt. James W. Severs, Company M; and Pvt. John R. Small, Company G — survived the valley and hilltop fights. The fourth, Pvt. John Sullivan, Company A, was killed at the river on the retreat. Seamans, Sullivan and Severs were all in their early 20s; only Small, at age 42, was older than Sivertsen. Pitsch believes the spectacles would have more likely belonged to an older man, such as Sivertsen or Small.

Sivertsen looms as the likely choice for another compelling reason — his previous occupation as a blacksmith. Among Pitsch's finds are numerous items related to that occupation. "A crucial artifact is a farrier style hammer of the common variety that a blacksmith might have carried," he says. In addition, he found a farrier's rasp, a bag of unused horseshoe nails and two new shoes among the remains, just the type of objects a company farrier might have possessed.

Pitsch and Swanson theorize that the animal might have been seized by another soldier who was later killed, or, riderless, it crossed the first of three river bends before fire from warriors brought it down. That area today is heavily covered with sage brush and grass. Depending on what that vicinity looked like in 1876, the horse could easily have been overlooked by soldier and Indian participants in the battle.

While many of his finds were displayed in his museum, his collection still needs to be studied more closely. Crucial would be to conduct firearms identifications of cases and bullets to determine if any match weapons used elsewhere during the battle. Because the valley sites have been used for multiple purposes since 1876, weeding out true battle artifacts from other historical or modern debris remains to be done. Pitsch points out, for example, "On the Timber Fight Line itself you have actually three different types of activities. You have the actual battle, then you have Gibbon's and Terry's camp, debris from that, and then you also have the areas that are kind of another dump site where they destroyed guns, burned saddles and the like."

He adds, "There is lots of work still to be done."

Scott, impressed with the quality of Pitsch's efforts, concluded in his report, "There is little doubt Mr. Pitsch's finds and detailed recording are a significant contribution to the Little Bighorn battle data base."

In an interview, Scott added, "A rigorous examination of that stuff will sort out some pieces, but there is no question that what he has on display at the museum at the present time is of the period. The context certainly suggests they were battle-related."

So much has changed in the interpretation of the various phases of the Battle of Little Bighorn since the archeological inquiries began in 1983, it would seem foolish to conclude that the final act has been written for these efforts. Not when Pitsch continues to search his land. Not when the tantalizing mystery of Deep Ravine and Company E still beckons for an answer that may come with a future technology. Scott originally intended to explore the area around each of the individual marble markers on the battlefield, a task that remains incomplete at this writing. The site of the proposed Indian memorial on a knoll adjacent to Last Stand Hill also must be studied before construction begins. Of course, the battlefield itself at any time may offer an unexpected artifactual discovery that could lead to a small inquiry or something larger. Undoubtedly, archeology will write several more chapters about what happened along the Little Bighorn in 1876.

Author s Note:

In early 1998, the Reno Battlefield Museum encountered financial problems and was closed. Later, it was reported that Jason Pitsch was selling a large number of items from his collection. The museum building itself was later sold and was being used for unrelated commercial purposes in 2003.

Unfortunately, in the late 1990s, Jason Pitsch himself faced federal legal charges arising out of personal activities unrelated to his artifact collecting or his museum operation. While Pitsch's legal problems amount to a personal tragedy for himself and his family, this author believes that his artifactual discoveries and historical theories remain valid for consideration by students of the Little Bighorn battle.

ARTIFACTS FROM THE PITSCH DISCOVERIES

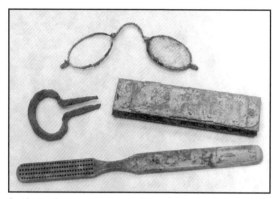

Artifacts that may have belonged to Cavalryman John Sivertsen. The toothbrush bears the initials "J.S."

A ring that is believed to bear the initials of Lt. Donald McIntosh, who was killed as he sought to escape from the timber, and his wife Mollie.

Saddle buckle fused, suggesting it was burned in a fire.

Match safe

All photos by Glen Swanson.

Indian spear point

ARTIFACTS FROM THE PITSCH DISCOVERIES

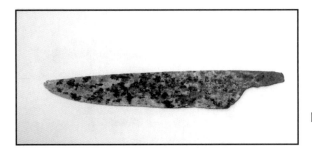

Indian knife

Arrowhead (top) and strike-a-light

Cavalry bugle bell and mouthpiece

ARTIFACTS FROM THE PITSCH DISCOVERIES

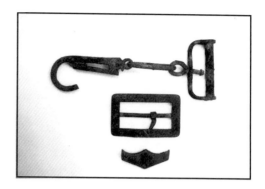

Springfield carbine hardware

**All photos by
Glen Swanson**

Indian crucifix

Religious medal from timber fight area

Chapter Eleven

THE INDIAN MEMORIAL

In my talks about George Custer and the Battle of the Little Bighorn, I always like to make one point clear. Only three facts are beyond controversy:
- Custer came to the Little Bighorn
- Custer saw the Little Bighorn
- The Indians conquered Custer at the Little Bighorn

Beyond that, everything else is open to debate. Controversy is guaranteed.

So it's not surprising that back in 1990-1991, the twin issues of renaming what had long been known as Custer battlefield, or some variation thereof, and the creation of a memorial to the Indian combatants stirred up a huge fuss. To Custer devotees, such as noted authors-researchers Lawrence Frost and John M. Carroll, the prospect of a name change to a more neutral Little Bighorn Battlefield National Monument was nothing less than sacrilege.

For many people, the idea that battlefields aren't named after individuals, especially the loser, seemed irrelevant. Calling Custer a loser also was hurtful; such a designation downplayed his fighting record during the Civil War. That American Indians today find the Custer name shameful made little difference. From just about the day after the fighting ended, the historic site had been known as Custer Battlefield.

A modern journalism axiom holds that names make news — and battlefield designations, too. That undoubtedly was true in 1876. Back then, everyone admired George Custer, a genuine hero since the Civil War— except, of course, American Indians whom he had been fighting. But they were in the minority. Besides, it is

Digging Into Custer's Last Stand

The extension of Battle Ridge has been an open prairie slope beyond the tour road that slipped around the 7th Cavalry Monument over the grave of the cavalrymen killed in battle in 1876. Now the new Indian Memorial is tucked into the ridgeline. Prior to the memorial's construction, some people worried that it would disturb the historic sightline, but on June 25, 2003, when it was dedicated, many observers expressed surprise at how well it fits into the landscape. The two memorials coexist well.

(Sandy Barnard)

well-established American tradition and political belief that the majority gets to name the field.

Thus, the battlefield became an historical Mecca for whites. Last Stand Hill beckoned with its granite obelisk that had stood on the grave of the enlisted men buried beneath it in 1881. In 1890, marble markers placed around the field designated where soldiers had presumably been killed or at least buried. The Indian dead all had been removed as soon as the fighting ceased, so recountings of the battle focused on the deeds of the soldiers, personified by the individual markers. Not surprisingly, across the many decades prior to the 1960s, Indians tended to stay away from the battlefield, except for those who visited during key anniversary observances. On those occasions, decked out in their most colorful warrior finery, they played their expected roles.

For example, nothing could have been more stirring than the 50th anniversary observance of the battle in 1926. Five companies of the modern 7th U.S. Cavalry Regiment arrived from Fort Bliss, Texas, bringing their horses in special cars arranged by the Burlington Quincy Railroad. A large contingent of Sioux and Cheyenne also arrived on horseback. The 7th marched on horseback across the field where their predecessors had fought and died. Seventh Cavalry veterans of the fight, including Brig. Gen Edward S. Godfrey, met with their surviving Indian opponents. Godfrey and Sitting Bull's nephew, White Bull, also a battle participant, exchanged gifts and officially "buried the hatchet."

Thus, for 70 or 80 years, story-telling at Custer Battlefield moved according to its own proper order and context. Custer came, he saw, and something happened to cause his defeat — but it all was quite glorious and historical.

166

For members of the Indian tribes who gathered at Little Bighorn on the dedication day for the Indian Memorial, June 25, 2003, the event offered an opportunity for traditional events and solemn observances. Many men, dressed in the garb of warriors, relived the ways of their ancestors in ceremonies on the ridge that stretched beyond the battlefield's Last Stand Hill.

(Sandy Barnard)

Yet as long ago as 1925, a few individuals thought the battle tales might be a tad one-sided: Custer always "lost," but that wasn't necessarily because the Indians had "won." On July 27, 1925, 11 months before the 50th anniversary commemoration, an Indian woman named Nellie Beaverheart undoubtedly had no idea that many years later she might be seen as a kind of rebel whose simple request, the first recorded for an Indian memorial of some kind, might unleash big changes at the battlefield. She wrote to the battlefield superintendent asking the War Department, which then had administrative control over the historic site, to mark the spot where her father, Lame White Man, had been killed:

"My father Vehoenxne was among the Cheyennes who was killed at the Custer Battle. He was a Cheyenne Chief and there are two Cheyenne men living who know where he fell and where he was buried. We would be glad if you could help us get the places marked, so that the place might be remembered on the next anniversary."[1]

Such a memorial at the battlefield would be a long time coming. It wasn't until the 1960s that American Indians, having viewed successes of African Americans through the Civil Rights Movement, began lobbying for change at Custer Battlefield. Not much happened until well in to the 1970s, so it wasn't surprising that in 1976, the centennial year of the Battle of Little Bighorn, controversy would rule the an-

An Indian-led color guard, consisting of veterans of various American military services during the country's recent wars, played a prominent role in the dedication ceremonies for the Indian Memorial on June 25, 2003.

(Sandy Barnard)

niversary ceremonies. As Edward Linenthal wrote in his book, *Sacred Ground*, "After the occupation of Alcatraz and the drama of Native American protest at Wounded Knee, South Dakota, the confluence of the centennial of the battle of Little Bighorn and the nation's bicentennial offered a perfect opportunity for Native Americans to dramatize the sins of Anglo-American culture by focusing on the infamy of one of the nation's great martial heroes."[2]

The 1976 ceremony, which at one time was expected to match the gaiety and hope for reconciliation that had marked the 1926 observances, was instead held amid concerns that violence might occur. The event was muted, attended by perhaps 800 people. Notably, the grandnephew of Custer, George Armstrong Custer III, played no official part in the event.

"Native Americans not only attacked the symbol of Custer at its source but planned their own ceremonies that were designed to celebrate a different reading of the battle," Linenthal stated.[3]

While violence was avoided, the 1976 event demonstrated that any notion of healing the traditional clash of cultures was set back for at least a generation. Custer's name would remain attached to the site and no monument to the Indians would be possible for the foreseeable future. Additionally, those who supported Custer and, by extension, the battlefield itself lost confidence in the National Park Service.

Linenthal summarized the situation this way:

"The struggle over the proper name for the battlefield was an important ongoing battle in the war for symbolic dominance at the Little Bighorn. For those who did not perceive the place as a shrine to Custer, and who believed the unfortunate fixation on him for the past century had contributed to continuing tension between cultures, the name change symbolized the beginning of the end of the age of Anglo-American dominance of the battlefield. For patriotic guardians, the attempt to change the name was one further example of the weakening of nurturing and sustaining American traditions, another in a series of perhaps irreparable blows to the cultural heroes of the nation."[4]

Although the question of a name change had been discussed for years, Linenthal notes that interest in erecting an Indian monument on the battlefield had been sporadic.[5] The absence of such a monument was intensified because most visitors perceived the 7th Cavalry grave marker as a memorial honoring Custer and his soldiers. The NPS periodically would state that the marker honored all participants, but, of course, Indian visitors clearly viewed it differently. Into the 1980s, the subject hovered in the background, while no formal action was taken.

Indian veteran stands at attention prior to the official ceremony dedicating the Indian Memorial at Little Bighorn Battlefield National Monument

(Cliff Hamby)

That changed on June 25, 1988, the battle's 112th anniversary, when Indian activist Russell Means and his followers in the American Indian Movement forced the issue. After a battlefield prayer service as part of American Indian International Peace Day, Means and his people removed a square-yard of sod near the base of the 7th Cavalry Monument, poured a frame of pre-mix cement and laid a plaque over it. The inscription, provocative in its phrasing, stated: "In honor of our Indian Patriots who fought and defeated the U.S. Calvary [sic]. In order to save our women and children from mass-murder. In doing so, preserving rights to our Homelands, Treaties and sovereignty. 6/25/1988 G. Magpie Cheyenne."

169

Digging Into Custer's Last Stand

The Spirit Warrior Sculpture is an eye-catching feature of the new Indian Memorial. In the background, through the area of the Spirit Gate, can be seen the historic 7th U.S. Cavalry Monument, erected in 1881 over the grave of the soldiers killed in battle on June 25-26, 1876.
(Sandy Barnard)

The move angered supporters of Custer and the 7th Cavalry, who criticized the NPS and Supt. Dennis Ditmanson for not preventing what they viewed as an illegal action and an affront to the memory of the soldiers. As Linenthal noted, "Means and his group…had escalated symbolic guerrilla warfare beyond protest at ritual events to physical intrusion at a patriotic gravesite."[6]

Despite the underlying anger and hostility on both sides as a result of Means's action, clearly he had forced the issue. While the plaque itself was removed in September 1988 and placed inside the museum in the Visitors Center, NPS Director William Penn Mott Jr. ordered that an Indian memorial committee be appointed to select a theme for the monument, organize a national competition for its design, and determine possible locations for its placement on the battlefield. The committee, which included historian Robert Utley and Means, set the memorial's theme as "Peace through Unity" and recommended that the memorial be placed on Custer Hill.

Two years later, in April 1990, Montana U.S. Representatives Ron Marlenee and Pat Williams and Colorado Rep. Ben Nighthorse Campbell (now U.S. senator), the only Native American member of the U.S. Congress, cosponsored a bill during the 101st Congress to erect an Indian memorial at the battlefield. The initial bill died when Williams sought to attach a provision for changing the battlefield name to Little Bighorn, but public hearings were ordered to gather information on both issues, the memorial and the name change. Critics complained that no monument for the Indian participants, who were viewed as the enemy in 1876, should be paid for by the U.S. government. They cited analogies about monuments for the Japanese at Pearl Harbor, Mexicans at the Alamo and Confederates on Civil War battlefields. Proponents noted that many Civil War battlefields have received federal funding for building Confederate memorials.

Linenthal cites a Missourian, who wrote that Confederate generals and soldiers are honored at Shiloh, Antietam and Chickamauga battlefields, even though they fought to preserve slavery or state sovereignty.

The man asked, "Are native Americans who fell in defense of their freedom, their way of life and their ancient homeland less worthy of respect given by fair historical treatment?"[7]

In public hearings in Billings, Mont., and Washington, D.C., debate covered a number of issues, including whether the historical generation of military men intended for the battlefield to bear Custer's name. Douglas C. McChristian, then chief historian at the battlefield, noted that Lt. Edward Maguire, Brig. Gen. Alfred H. Terry's engineering officer, had used "Custer Battlefield" on his early map of the area to distinguish it from Major Marcus A. Reno's battlefield four miles away. For Maguire, McChristian reported, the surrounding battlefield area was designated as Little Bighorn.[8]

On Dec. 10, 1991, Public Law 102-201 was enacted, officially changing the name of the historic site to Little Bighorn Battlefield National Monument. In addition, it established a committee to advise the secretary of the interior, who oversees the NPS, on the task of establishing an Indian memorial at Little Bighorn. Pointedly, no funding was provided by this enabling legislation.

Eleven months later, on Veterans Day, Nov. 11, 1992, the National Park Service marked the change of name with a ceremony. On a cold and snowy day, only about 1,000 people attended, but they included descendants of Crazy Horse, Sitting Bull and Dewey Beard, who had been the last surviving warrior. Keynote speaker Lionel Bordeaux, president of Sinte Gleska University on the Rosebud Sioux Reservation in South Dakota, said the name change "represented the native Americans' second victory at the Little Bighorn, 'the victory of the people who worked so hard to see that this place is called by its rightful name'."

INDIAN MEMORIAL REALIZED

As is always true at Little Bighorn, the final steps that brought the memorial into existence were not without controversy. In 1994, then-Secretary of Interior Bruce Babbitt appointed an Indian Memorial Advisory Committee, made up of members from the Indian nations involved in the battle, historians, artists and landscape architects.

In 1996, the National Park Service, guided by the advisory committee, conducted a national design competition that drew 554 submissions. In 1997, the entry submitted by John Collins and Allison Powers, a husband and wife team from Philadelphia, was selected as the winner. The sub-committee that reviewed the entries consisted of Arthur Amiotte, a Sioux artist and adjunct professor of native studies and art at Brandon University; Paul Andrew Hutton, professor of history at the University of New Mexico; A. Gay Kingman, Lakota educator and director of public relations for the National Indian Gaming Association; Richard Pohl, a landscape architect at Montana State University, Bozeman; Crow artist Kevin Red Star; Carol Redcherries, chief justice for the Northern Cheyenne Appellate Court;

Digging Into Custer's Last Stand

and Northern Arapaho architect Dennis Sun Rhodes of AmerINDIAN Architecture in St. Paul, Minnesota.[9]

Collins, a landscape architect who apparently had never visited the Little Bighorn Battlefield, told the *Philadelphia Enquirer* that he was attracted by the prizes offered in this competition. Their entry's low-key and simple characteristics had much to do with its selection. As Collins explained it in media accounts, he wanted to make "large gestures" and deliberately left some features ambiguous.[10]

Rules for the design competition stressed that the Indian memorial should not compete directly with the 7th Cavalry Monument, but the two should relate to each other. The Collins-Powers design was shaped around the open, circular plaza, which would serve as a "gathering place." The surrounding earthen berm simulates an elemental landform in keeping with ancient earthworks found in North America.

Thus, the final design incorporated a circular earthen and stone structure carved into the prairie, commemorating the five tribes who fought there: the Lakota, Cheyenne and Arapaho who defeated the 7th Cavalry under Lt. Col. George Custer, and the Crow and Arikara scouts who guided Custer. A weeping wall was added symbolizing the tears and suffering of Indian people and the interior walls will be permanently inscribed with stories of the tribes who participated in the battle. The 7th Cavalry Monument may be viewed across the tour road through a "spirit

Interior of the Indian Memorial, June 2003, with the 7th Cavalry
Monument in center rear

(Cliff Hamby)

gate." Opposite the spirit gate, framed against the sloping ridge, is a sculpture of three large-scale silhouette figures of Sioux, Cheyenne and Arapaho spirit warriors mounted on galloping horses and a woman handing a shield to one of them as they prepare for battle. Designed by Canadian Indian artist Colleen Cutschall, it was inspired by Indian ledger art.

The slightly ghostly figures, Collins told the *Enquirer*, recall the two-dimensional pictographs Indian tribes used to record their history.[11] Eventually, two 30-foot poles with fluttering pennants are to straddle the gap and form a spirit gate, not for the passage of modern-day visitors to the battlefield, but rather to welcome the cavalry dead and signify mutual understanding.[12]

Unfortunately, at the time the design was selected, not enough money had been raised to build the memorial. Efforts to secure private donations, including Indian sources, failed. In 1998, after Neil Mangum was appointed the battlefield's superintendent, he made building the memorial his personal priority. When donations lagged, he took the controversial step of increasing entrance fees for the battlefield and dedicating those funds for its construction.

Equally important, he also lobbied hard for federal funding. In September 2001, Congress approved an Interior appropriations bill that included $2.3 million for the Indian Memorial. Construction began on April 23, 2002, with completion slated for that fall. Initially, Mangum considered dedicating the memorial that November, but a summer date of June 25, 2003, was eventually chosen.

Now, on the lonely edge of what has long been known as Battle Ridge, the new memorial stands 75 yard northeast of Last Stand Hill, just across the battlefield tour road from the 7th Cavalry's granite obelisk.

THE DEDICATION CEREMONY

On the day of the battle in 1876, June 25 was blistering hot, with temperatures near 100 degree. The ceremony changing the battlefield's name occurred in the midst of winter-like weather in 1992, but for the dedication of the Indian Memorial at Little Bighorn on June 25, 2003, things could not have been more perfect. June 25, 2003, was cool and pleasant. Each time the sun threatened too much warmth, clouds intervened to keep temperatures comfortable as a crowd estimated at between 4,000-5,000 people gathered for the mostly Indian-led ceremonies. Also attending were assorted levels of elected and appointed government officials, including U.S. Secretary of the Interior Gale Norton, U.S. Sen. Ben Nighthorse Campbell, R-Colo., and Montana Gov. Judy Martz. Numerous American Indian leaders, such as Leland Spotted Bird (Fort Peck Sioux), Geri Small (Northern Cheyenne) and Carl Venne (Crow) also participated. Not invited to be part of the official program, Russell Means nonetheless inserted himself into the event. Even a reenactment unit of Buffalo Soldiers added to the diversity of the occasion.

Oglala Sioux healer George Amiotte recalled for the news media how on June 25, 2003, he came alone at daybreak to pray at the new Indian Memorial at Little Bighorn Battlefield, before the thousands of visitors began to arrive for the dedication ceremonies later that day.[13]

Leland Spotted Bird, council member for the Fort Peck Assinibione and Sioux Tribes, raises his staff after concluding his remarks to the crowd gathered in the amphitheater of the battlefield on June 25, 2003. Behind him is Lois Red Elk, an actress and tribal member of the Fort Peck Tribes.
(Cliff Hamby)

He prayed for the dead of the three warrior societies to which he belongs on the Pine Ridge Reservation in South Dakota, in thanks for their sacrifice. As he told a *Billings Gazette* reporter, Amiotte is a member of the same warrior society that claims Crazy Horse and knows a little about the courage it took to fight at the Little Bighorn. Amiotte wore, pinned to his vest, the four Purple Hearts and a Bronze Star he earned during three tours of duty with the U.S. Marines in Vietnam.

The *Billings Gazette* story noted: "Amiotte didn't pray alone for long, especially after relatives saw what he was doing. Soon he was in the middle of a circle of hundreds of Sioux, Cheyenne, Arapaho, Crow and Arikara who followed his lead in honoring their dead. He recalled that before charging the 7th Cavalry's positions in 1876, Lakota warriors encouraged each other by noting that it was a good day to die."

"Today is a beautiful day to be alive in the great circle of life," Amiotte exhorted the modern crowd. "Remember the beauty of their deaths. Make the warriors who laid down their lives proud of you."[14]

174

Another Indian participant-onlooker was Donovin Sprague, a Rapid City historian and college teacher. He pointed out a rocky flat spot down in Deep Ravine where it is believed his great-great-grandfather Hump was shot in the leg. As Sprague told the *Rapid City Journal*, Hump — the name refers to the high backbone of a buffalo — had fought alongside Crazy Horse all the way up Deep Ravine from the huge Indian camp on the Little Bighorn River. Despite a leg wound from a soldier's bullet, the young Minneconjou warrior kept fighting. He reached the top of Calhoun Hill, where Lt. James Calhoun's Company L was overrun.[15]

Sprague cited a special reason for attending the dedication ceremonies. His family recently had also named him Hump, the third Minneconjou to bear that name in the past 150 years, so he was on hand to represent his great-great-grandfather Hump.

"I feel proud that our people were able to defend themselves and their families," said Sprague, who comes to the battlefield often.

The vast majority of the people who attended were from the Sioux, Cheyenne, Arapaho, Crow and Arikara tribes — the historic groups who fought in the legendary encounter. On that day they gathered on what they viewed as sacred ground, earned by the blood of their ancestors protecting their respective people.

Battlefield Supt. Darrell Cook found himself proud for a couple of reasons. Administratively, he was in charge of the day's events, which required months of behind-the-scenes preparations. One area was certainly law enforcement, given the number of uniformed law enforcement personnel in conspicuous view. Reportedly, a number of plains-clothed officers mixed with the crowds.

In addition, Cook is a relative of Dewey Beard, the last surviving participant in the Little Bighorn clash as well as a survivor of the armed conflict between the Army and the Lakota at Wounded Knee, S.D., in 1890.

"People have been saying that this event closes the circle. No, it doesn't," Cook said. "Installing a memorial was a big step, but there is a lot more to do. We need to bring more balance to the larger story."[16]

Probably the most poignant moment of the whole daylong ceremonies took place when the family members of fallen soldier Private First Class Lori Piestewa were honored. Piestewa, a 23-year-old Hopi woman, was killed in March 2003 during

Former Supt. Neil Mangum (L) and U.S. Sen. Ben Nighthorse Campbell (2nd from R) played instrumental roles in the creation of an Indian Memorial at Little Bighorn Battlefield. Between them is another former superintendent, Gerard Baker. At the far right is Burton Two Leggins of the Crow tribe.

(Cliff Hamby)

Montana Gov. Judy Martz (L) and U.S. Interior Secretary Gale Norton were among the official dignataries who spoke at the dedication.
(Cliff Hamby)

an ambush in Iraq and was the first American Indian woman to die in combat with American military forces. Her mother, father, husband and two children traveled from Tuba City, Ariz., to attend the ceremonies and were introduced by Montana Governor Martz, who greeted the family with hugs and kisses.

"You have given us the ultimate price," the governor told the fallen soldier's family."[17]

Piestewa's mother told the *Billings Gazette*, "The Native American people have been so supportive of us and our family in the hardest time of our lives. When they invited us we felt we owed them to come for all the support they've given us. We're very honored to be here."

Besides Martz, other invited politicians had their moments during the formal program, saying just about what you might expect on such occasions. President George Bush did not attend, as some had speculated he might. In his place appeared Interior Secretary Gale Norton, whose department oversees both the National Park Service and the Bureau of Indian Affairs.

"Since 1881, there has been a monument to General Custer and his soldiers. Consecrated in this same ground is the blood of Native Americans, the great Sioux Nation, the Northern Cheyenne and Arapaho, and the scouting tribes, Crow and Arikara," the secretary said. "And yet for 127 years, no monument marked their loss of life. We are here today to change that."

Norton invoked the wisdom of Black Elk, a Lakota holy man who as a 13-year-old witnessed the fighting in 1876 and later became a leading spokesman for peace and healing in Anglo-Indian relations. "We cannot change or reclaim the past. The

Indian activist Russell Means may have crashed the memorial dedication party, so to speak, but his remarks at a few points seemed surprisingly conciliatory to many observers.
(Sandy Barnard)

wrongs, the battles, the broken promises remain as they were written into history. Yet we are able to take another step together to seek the peace that Black Elk spoke of many decades ago," Norton continued. "The essential irony of the Battle of the Little Bighorn is the victors who defeated Custer and the 7th Cavalry would soon lose their own traditional way of life."[18]

Speaking to the audience gathered in the amphitheater below the Custer National Cemetery by the Visitors Center, Norton noted, "By confronting our past and looking to the future, we are healing our wounds. Those wounds were immensely deep."

In his comments U.S. Senator Nighthorse Campbell, undoubtedly the most influential national politician behind the move for the Indian Memorial, reminded the audience that the United States in 1881 had built a monument to the soldiers who died there, but none for the victorious Indians. It should have been done before, Campbell said, "but today it's done."

He said Indians suffered many injustices, including not getting the right to vote until 1927. "This brings one little part to closure," Campbell told the crowd.[19]

For his part, Campbell suggested to the crowd that "History is sometimes distorted by the winners of a battle," but that the Indian Memorial was an "effort to give equal honor and equal dignity to all the warriors who were involved."

His comment about the battle winners appeared odd, as he presumably meant to criticize the traditional white historical accounts that told of the glory of the Custer and the 7th Cavalry while he praised the victorious Indians, whose views went unconsidered for 100 years or more.

After his public remarks, Campbell told the *Rocky Mountain News*, "For me, being here is like having the rebirth of something in you that should have stayed alive all these years, but didn't. This really is a holy area for me."[20]

Digging Into Custer's Last Stand

Numerous Indian leaders were invited to speak, but one man not on the guest list commandeered the stage and caught the public's attention. Indian activist Russell Means bounced to the stage for an impromptu but impassioned speech.

"I want to tell you a little bit of the history here before the government revises it," Means, wearing a bright red shirt, began. As he spoke, however, some of the politicians left the stage, including Governor Martz and Secretary Norton. Senator Campbell remained, standing and, at times, smiling softly.

Means, in a reference to Campbell, quipped, "Now even the Republicans are down here!" he said. "That's prestigious!"

To the surprise of many who thought Means might be disruptive, he appeared conciliatory, despite calling the memorial to 7th Cavalry troopers, "the phallic symbol up on the hill." Means claimed that, if he had known that the 7th Cavalry monument represented a mass grave, he would have placed his handmade plaque elsewhere in 1988. He continued that after he visited the battlefield in 1970, he had a vision that a memorial to the Indians would be erected.

Speaking emotionally, Means told the audience, "I want to thank you for being here to honor my culture and my people."

He noted that AIM had "put 'American' before our ethnicity," Means said. "By putting ethnicity first, that's where your mind goes. That's where your heart goes."

He pointed out, "The memorial is not about war. It's not to remember war." Noting the new memorial's position along battlefield ridge, he added, "The last thing you'll remember when you're leaving is us."

Representatives of the modern 7th U.S. Cavalry participated in the ceremonies by carrying the colors.
(Sandy Barnard)

According to the symbolism underscoring the Indian Memorial, the Weeping Wall with its pool ties together the two monuments that stand opposite each other on Battle Ridge.
(Sandy Barnard)

MEANING OF THE INDIAN MEMORIAL

The historical story of the American West is both messy and complicated, so it is not surprising that it is often viewed from a variety of perspectives. For most Native Americans, the West involves colonialism and conquest as well as a life of agency and adaptation under tremendously difficult circumstances. For Anglo-Americans (mislabeled because most did not originate in England), the so-called Indian wars are seen as a necessary and glorious part of the country's fulfillment of its destiny, of people overcoming dangers and hardships to build a better life.

Not surprisingly, ever since the first guns fired to open the Battle of Little Bighorn in 1876, the battlefield itself has been about this clash of cultures. The 1876 fighting itself involved violent confrontation, of course, but over the years, a continuing dispute in words, beliefs and concerns has been waged, often in the most subtle of ways.

For example, this clash continues in the labels applied to depictions of their respective cultures. Among the crowd at the 2003 ceremonies were many Indians dressed in traditional costumes, there to honor their ancestors. These Indians were viewed as faithfully living out their ancestral traditions and customs. In contrast, white and black men dressed in the garb of the 19th century American cavalrymen were labeled "reenactors," mere actors on the broad stage of the Little Bighorn.

A similar dichotomy could be seen in the ways the two cultures approached their ceremonies. Citing their religious underpinnings, the Indians refused to let their ceremonies be photographed; during the memorial dedication, mounted men on horseback challenged anyone who dared to raise a camera toward where the

179

dancers and drummers were performing. Although some non-Indians expressed concerned about such threatening behavior, no law enforcement officers, at least in uniform, were visible. Reportedly, some in plainclothes stood by.

In contrast, the more official events in the public amphitheater and elsewhere on the field were photographed openly by the public and the news media. Religion was mentioned in a public sort of way, but no one seemed to believe that the spirits of Custer and his men still walked the ground where they had been violently dispatched in combat in 1876. Wherever one looked, armed law enforcement officers could be seen.

Not a few people criticized the NPS for its failure to treat both sides equally. As one man said, "How can you have a closed religious ceremony on a public historic site paid for and maintained by my dollars and those of every American taxpayer? And, then allow those thugs to treat taxpayers that way."

That June, NPS officials avoided answering the question directly.

The difference between the cultures also could be seen in the way the two races approach the Indian Memorial. "To Native Americans this memorial is the first time in the history of the United States of America that aboriginal people are being recognized through governmental processes," said William C. Hair, a Northern Arapaho. "This is the closest we'll ever come to acknowledgment from the government of the atrocities we have suffered."[21]

Senator Campbell and many other native participants saw the historical Indians as patriots. "Clearly, the Indian people of the time were defending their God-given rights," Hair said.[22]

"The monument is appropriate," said Kevin J. Connelly, president of the Custer Battlefield Historical and Museum Association.

Some CBHMA members initially opposed the memorial, but the organization itself donated funds for its construction. "Some think there could have been a better place for it, but for the most part our members accept it," Connolly told the *Wall Street Journal*. "The fight is over."[23]

Speakers and spectators alike hailed the new Indian Memorial. "I have a feeling of pride. This unity is a healing power," said Anthony Littlewhirlwind of Great Falls, Mont., a descendant of Littlewhirlwind, a Cheyenne warrior who died in the battle.[24]

Just two months before, David Little Wounded, 20, of Dupree, S.D., learned that he is related to two key battle figures.

"The memorial is important to me because I'm related to both Crazy Horse and Sitting Bull," Little Wounded said.[25]

In his opening address at the dedication, Crow Tribal Chairman Carl Venne said, "Today, I am proud to be an American."

Gerald Sherman, Roscoe, Mont., not surprisingly liked the memorial. His cousin, Colleen Cutschall, designed the Spirit Warriors' sculpture.

"I think it's great that this monument is there for the Indian people," Sherman said.

As he stood by the Spirit Warriors sculpture, Herbert Bear Chum Sr. said the memorial would remind people "that we are still here. Never forget."[26]

Ernie LaPointe, a great-grandson of Sitting Bull, saw irony in what subsequently happened to the victors and the vanquished. "The only ones who ever had a monument here were the ones who lost the battle," he said.[27]

But on the day of the ceremony, he also appreciated the similarities between the combatants on both sides. These had overtaken their differences in his mind.

"To me, this is all hallowed ground; you can feel the spirits of those that died here. The 7th Cavalry, the Indians, they're here together now. To me, this monument is an honor to all the fallen warriors."[28]

Brothers Floyd and Delmar Clown of the Cheyenne River Indian Reservation are descendants of Crazy Horse's family. They gave the memorial design mixed reactions, saying it did not reflect Lakota traditions. For example, they said, the memorial shows a chief leading warriors into battle. Traditionally, chiefs weren't the first into battle, Floyd Clown said.

"Even though the design is not Lakota, they're honoring our grandfathers and grandmothers who were here," Clown said. "It's good they made a gesture like this. This memorial is to the Lakota people."[29]

Two ideas seemed to predominate that day among the Indians. One that they had won a great victory at the Little Bighorn on June 25, 1876, and two, that they are a great people who remain vibrant, despite the hardships they have endured.

"I never thought it [Indian Memorial] was going to happen," said Donlin Many Bad Horses, a Northern Cheyenne. "But today it did happen and I'm very glad so many people came out — came out to see what kind of people we are, the proud people we are."[30]

Reenactors depicting warriors and soldiers played an active part officially and unofficially in the ceremonies that took place on Little Bighorn Battlefield on June 25, 2003.
(Cliff Hamby)

Digging Into Custer's Last Stand

THE HORSE CEMETERY

When plans were being made to construct the Indian Memorial near Last Stand Hill, battlefield staff members realized work on related sidewalks might impact the nearby site where in 1881 skeletal remains of 7th Cavalry horses were buried during installation of the 7th Cavalry Monument. Sidewalk construction specifications and terrain constraints required removing two or more feet of dirt and disturbing the subsurface up to a depth of four feet to install retaining walls for the memorial.

Arrangements were made for an archeological study from April 29 to May, 1, 2002, of what had long been referred to as the horse cemetery. The team, once again led by Douglas D. Scott, NPS Midwest Archeological Center, included Thomas Thiessen, Harold Roeker and Wilfred Husted. Fortunately, his investigation determined the horse pit lay outside of the construction zone for the Indian Memorial.

According to research by Chief Historian John Doerner, the 7th Cavalry horse cemetery had been rediscovered on April 9, 1941, by NPS maintenance personnel excavating for an overflow water drainage pipeline which ran from the old water reservoir tank on Custer Hill.[31] The 20,000-gallon tank lay buried on the northeast side of Last Stand Hill, immediately east of the 7th Cavalry Monument. The tank's date of construction is not unknown, but Doerner's research put it about 1911. Water was pumped to the tank from the Little Bighorn River, and, in turn, delivered by

Roger Hoffman, Pierre, S.D., stood ramrod straight throughout the ceremony dedicating a marker, seen at the left, over the site of the horse burial pit on Last Stand Hill.

(Sandy Barnard)

gravity fed lines to the National Cemetery irrigation system and to a hypochlorinater that filtered the water for the drinking fountain and NPS residences.

In an April 18, 1941, letter to the U.S. Quartermaster General, Supt. Edward S. Luce wrote:

"While digging an excavation the East End of the wooden trench or 'horse cemetery' on Custer Hill was encountered. The wooden end of the trench gave way and about ten horse skeletons fell out. Among these bones were human bones. They were the leg and arm bones, but no skulls. There was also a pair of cavalry trooper's boots with a few toe bones inside. The tin cracker boxes: 'C.L.Woodman & Co., Chicago,' with bullet holes through the tin were found. These at one time contained 'hardtack' and were used for protection as breastworks during the fight on Custer Hill, at the time when General Custer ordered all the horses shot to form protection for a defensive position....This horse trench was not thoroughly explored...The grave or trench has been closed waiting instructions from your office...."

In an April 9, 1941, letter to his superiors at Yellowstone National Park, Luce reported, inaccurately, the cemetery may have measured 50 by 20 feet. Luce also noted:

"In a cavalry regiment there is a great attachment between the rider and his horse and there is not doubt that due reverence and respect were shown these horses when they were buried in 1877. For this reason it is requested that permission be given to properly outline this 'horse cemetery' with an fenced-in enclosure and have a historic sign made that will explain to the tourists and visitors to this cemetery of the prominent part played by these horses in the battle and the sacrifice they made for the protection of their riders."

Such a marking of the horse cemetery would not occur until the summer of 2003. Its origins date to the immediate post-battle years. In his first visit to Last Stand Hill two days after the battle, Lt. Edward S. Godfrey, Company K, observed, "There were 42 men and 39 dead horses on Custer Hill."

Lt. Edward J. McClernand, attached to the Montana Column, made similar statements: "On top of Custer Hill was a circle of dead horses with a 30 foot diameter, which was not badly formed. Around Custer some 30 or 40 men had fallen, some of whom had evidently used their horses as breastworks."

Finally, Col. John Gibbon noted: "Numerous dead horses were lying along the southwestern slope of Custer Hill. On the very top were found four or five dead horses which were swollen, putrid, and offensive, their stiffened legs sticking straight out from their bodies. Close under the brow of the hill several horses are lying together, and by the side of one of these Custer was found."

These and other historic accounts make it clear that in 1876 the burials of the dead soldiers were hasty and cursory at best. In the next few years, natural erosion, animal action and some human vandalism led to frequent reports of human skeletal remains laying exposed on the battlefield. In 1877, 1879 and 1881, Army burial parties reinterred remains exposed by the elements and scavengers. During these projects, the first photographs known to have been taken on Last Stand Hill, one by John Fouch in 1877 and others by Stanley J. Morrow in 1879, also showed heavy concentrations of horse bones still strewn over the field.

Digging Into Custer's Last Stand

During the 1879 effort, an Army detachment carefully remounded what were believed to be the graves of Custer's men. In addition, stakes were placed at what were presumed to have been the original 7th Cavalry death sites. At that time, the skeletal remains of cavalry horses were placed inside an 11-foot cordwood monument erected on Custer Hill as a temporary memorial to the troopers.

Capt. G.K. Sanderson, 11th Infantry, from nearby Fort Custer, supervised the 1879 detail and reported:

"I accordingly built a mound...out of cordwood filled in the center of the mound with all the horse bones I could find on the field....This grave was then built up with wood for four feet above ground, well covered, and the mound built over and around it. The mound is ten feet square and about eleven feet high; is built on the highest point immediately in rear of where Gen'l Custer's body was found...Newspaper reports to the effect that bodies still lay exposed are sensational...I believe the large number of horse bones lying over the field have given rise to some of such statements, and to prevent any such statements being made in the future, I had all the horse bones gathered together and placed in the mound where they can not be readily disturbed by curiosity seekers."

Morrow, who was present with Sanderson's crew, took a series of historic photographs which clearly show the horse bones gathered on Custer Hill in several large piles just prior to their interment within the cordwood monument.

Two years later, in July 1881, Sanderson's cordwood monument was dismantled and a 36,000-pound granite memorial was erected in its place. Lt. Charles F. Roe, 2nd Cavalry, reported: "I placed the monument on the point of the hill within six (6) feet of the place where the remains of General Custer were found after the fight."

Roe makes no mention of removing the horse bones, but Doerner believes they were probably reinterred just to the northeast of the monument. He notes in his report, "The fond reverence that the cavalry held for their horses is evident in Luce's 1941 report which mentions the presence of original 1879 memorial cordwood that was utilized by Lt. Roe's 1881 detail to line the horse cemetery."

World War II delayed further excavation of the horse cemetery until July 1946, when Luce requested the assistance of Lt. Col. Elwood L. Nye, a U.S. Army veterinarian. No formal report on his 1946 work was apparently submitted.

In February 2002, prior to Scott's field work, the horse pit was relocated by comparing the modern landscape to photographs from 1941 and by a multi-instrument geophysical survey of the site using ground penetrating radar and electromagnetics and magnetometery.

Scott's excavation located horse remains in two areas, measuring roughly six feet square, just to the northeast of the 7th Cavalry Monument. The remains included a vertebra, leg bones, shoulder bone and rib bones. In a preliminary report, Scott wrote: "The pit was located to the west of the zone (Future Sidewalk) by a few feet. As it was outside the direct impact zone, but potentially within the AEC (Area of Excavation & Construction) it was decided in consultation with Superintendent Mangum, to document the feature and its contents in place and preserve the same in place. Notes, maps and photographs were taken or made to document the feature

7TH CAVALRY
HORSE CEMETERY

IN MEMORY OF
7TH CAVALRY HORSES
KILLED DURING
CUSTER'S LAST STAND
JUNE 25, 1876
AND LATER BURIED HERE
IN JULY 1881
UNDER SUPERVISION OF
LT. CHARLES F. ROE
OF THE 2ND CAVALRY

Sandy Barnard

and those bones and other items observed at the exposed surface. The feature was covered with plastic and backfilled. Wooden stakes were placed after backfilling to define the features boundaries so that construction work will not inadvertently impact the site."

Additionally, he concluded that Luce erred in his 1940s estimation of the cemetery's size. The pit Scott's team explored was only about 8 x 5 feet. Its depth was undetermined since it was not fully excavated. Scott suspects Luce exaggerated the size to gain support for further exploration of the site. Whether wood found in the pit actually came from the original cordwood monument also could not be determined. Instead, it may have come from a wooden cover placed over the pit.

His study also indicated that the site had been adversely affected after 1946 by later construction on Last Stand Hill. The water tank was removed in the early 1950s and the parking lot was paved in 1962. "If this supposition is correct, it seems likely that this mid-20th century disturbance seriously effected the feature and its contents, clearly breaking and abrading many of the exposed elements," he wrote in his report.

Finally, recovered bone elements indicated that a minimum of two horses had been buried there. "No doubt there are many more than that present, but only full excavation and analysis can answer the question," he concluded.

Scott believes the horse burials were likely done more as an expedient means of disposing of their remains rather than memorializing the animals. Thus, Doerner concluded it was time to honor the horses that had carried their riders from Fort Abraham Lincoln in Dakota Territory to the battlefield along the Little Bighorn River. So Doerner sought to have a permanent memorial erected over the burial site to recall the animals who died in battle with their riders.

"We don't often think of horses as making sacrifices in battle," Doerner noted, "but they too 'gave their all' during one of our nation's most famous battles."

On Sunday June 29, 2003, another ceremony was held on Last Stand Hill to dedicate both an interpretive wayside exhibit and a granite marker that pay homage to the 7th Cavalry horses interred there.

Endnotes

[1] "Superintendent's Notes," *The Battlefield Dispatch*, No. 4 (Hardin, Mont.: Custer Battlefield Historical and Museum Association), 9

[2] Edward Tabor Linenthal, *Sacred Ground, Americans and Their Battlefields* (Chicago: University of Illinois Press, 1993), 141

[3] Linenthal, 144

[4] Linenthal, 148

[5] Linenthal, 158

[6] Linenthal, 159-160

[7] Linenthal, 226

[8] Linenthal, 227-228

[9] Charles Rankin, "An Indian Memorial for Little Bighorn," *Montana The Magazine of Western History* (Helena: Montana Historical Society, Summer 1997), 58

[10] Rankin, 58

[11] Rankin, 58

[12] Rankin, 58

[13] *Billings (Mont.) Gazette,* June 26, 2003

[14] *Billings Gazette,* June 26, 2003

[15] *Rapid City (S.D.) Journal,* June 26, 2003

[16] *Christian Science Monitor,* June 24, 2003

[17] *Billings Gazette,* June 26, 2003

[18] *Salt Lake City (Utah) Tribune,* 6-26-03; *Rapid City Journal,* 6-26-03

[19] *Billings Gazette,* June 26, 2003

[20] *Rocky Mountain (Colo.) News,* June 26, 2003

[21] *Philadelphia Inquirer,* June 25, 2003

[22] *Rapid City Journal,* June 26, 2003

[23] *Wall Street Journal,* June 25, 2003

[24] *Rapid City Journal,* June 26, 2003

[25] *Rapid City Journal,* June 26, 2003

[26] *Denver Post,* June 26, 2003

[27] *Rocky Mountain News,* June 26, 2003

[28] *Rocky Mountain News,* June 26, 2003

[29] *Rapid City Journal,* June 26, 2003

[30] *Billings Gazette,* June 26, 2003

[31] Report provided to author by John Doerner, chief historian, Little Bighorn Battlefield National Monument, June 2003. It was drawn from a paper, "The Enduring Monument – The Enigma of Custer Hill," that he delivered Feb. 23, 2002, at the 6th Annual Denver Custer/Indian Wars Symposium, Denver, Colo. The information, used with his permission, is also posted on the web site of the Friends of the Little Bighorn Battlefield at *http://www.friendslittlebighorn.com/Horse%20Cemetery.htm.* In addition, the following report by Douglas D. Scott, chief archeologist at the Midwest Archeological Center, National Park Service, Lincoln, Neb., was used for this summary: "Archeological Investigations of the "Horse Cemetery" Site, Little Bighorn Battlefield National Monument," July 2002. It, too, is posted on the Friends web site at *http://www.friendslittlebighorn.com/Scott%20Horse%20Cemetery%20Report.htm.*

OTHER BOOKS BY SANDY BARNARD

Campaigning with the Irish Brigade: Pvt. John Ryan, 28th Massachusetts
(Terre Haute, Ind.: AST Press, 2001)

Ten Years with Custer, a 7th Cavalryman's Memoirs
(Terre Haute, Ind.: AST Press, 2001)

Custer's First Sergeant John Ryan
(Terre Haute, Ind.: AST Press, 1996)

Digging Into Custer's Last Stand
(Terre Haute, Ind.: AST Press, 1986, 1998)

I Go With Custer, The Life and Death of Reporter Mark Kellogg
(Bismarck, N.D.: Bismarck Tribune Publishing Co., 1996)

Shovels & Speculation, Archeologists Hunt Custer
(Terre Haute, Ind.: AST Press, 1990)

Speaking About Custer
(Terre Haute, Ind.: AST Press, 1991)

All may be ordered from:
AST Press
22 Todd Drive
Terre Haute, IN 47803
(812) 877-3691